THE WRITER'S GUIDE TO

The Comprehensive Guide to Building & Sustaining a Successful Career
Edited by Benjamin Sobieck

WD
WRITER'S DIGEST BOOKS

WritersDigest.com
Cincinnati, Ohio

For more resources for writers, visit www.writersdigest.com.

22 21 20 19 18   5 4 3 2 1

Distributed in the U.K. and Europe by F+W Media International
Pynes Hill Court, Pynes Hill, Rydon Lane
Exeter, EX2 5AZ, United Kingdom
Tel: (+44) 1392-797680, Fax: (+44) 1626-323319
E-mail: postmaster@davidandcharles.co.uk

Library of Congress Cataloging-in-Publication Data

ISBN-13: 978-1-4403-5293-5

Edited by Amy Jones
Designed by Alexis Estoye and Liz Harasymczuk
Production coordinated by Debbie Thomas

Dedication

For Jane

Acknowledgments

This book would not be possible without the marvelous teams at Writer's Digest and Wattpad. Many excellent people offered their time, talent, and, most importantly, trust to bring to life something that started as an idea on a scrap of paper. However, special recognition must be granted to two people in particular.

I-Yana Tucker at Wattpad worked with me in the trenches to make the wheels turn, often putting my own claims of being a night owl to shame. This wouldn't be the book it is without her contributions. I must also recognize Phil Sexton, who was the publisher of Writer's Digest when I pitched this book, for entertaining yet another of my wild ideas in the first place.

I need to acknowledge Wattpad user @StephanieTheWriter, who played an unintentional role. In 2015, when I was new to Wattpad, she chastised me for not posting more than the first few chapters of *Glass Eye: Confessions of a Fake Psychic Detective*. Had she not prodded me to keep posting, I wouldn't have gone on to do half of what's in my bio, and I probably wouldn't be writing these words. Thank you.

About the Editor

Benjamin Sobieck likes to say he's done a little of everything in the writing/publishing world except sweep the floors, although he's pretty sure he's done that, too. He's served for ten years as an editor and product manager for F+W Media, working with a variety of enthusiast books, magazines, TV shows, digital content, and e-commerce.

His *Confessions of a Fake Psychic Detective* novel trilogy on Wattpad won a Watty Award, the world's largest online fiction writing contest. As a member of the Wattpad Stars, he partnered on branded campaigns with FOX, Paramount Pictures, Universal Pictures, and many others. He is also the author of *The Writer's Guide to Weapons*, published by Writer's Digest Books, and offers a similar blog at crimefictionbook.com.

Ever the tinkerer, he is the creator of The Writer's Glove® (thewritersglove.com), used in nearly forty countries and featured by *Glamour* magazine. Sobieck lives in Minnesota with his wife and two children. His favorite color is blue, but Wattpad orange is a close second.

Table of Contents

Part 3: Building Your Writing Career

Stay True to Yourself

By Anna Todd

On Wattpad: @imaginator1D

Write a story that you believe in.

You've picked this book up for a reason. You want to be a writer, or you want to find a way to publish your work. First, congratulations on having the courage to take a step toward your dream! For some perspective about where this journey can lead you, let me tell you about my Wattpad experience.

STARTING SMALL IS STILL A START

Just four years ago, I was an Army wife sitting at Ft. Hood, Texas, going to community college (barely, I just wanted to feel like I was moving toward becoming an adult), and I had no idea what I wanted to do for a living. Writing for a living was a dream of mine, but it seemed so unrealistic. I didn't know anyone who had a book published, and I didn't even have a college degree. I used to think that mattered when it came to being a writer. Now I know that all it takes to be a writer, is to write. That's it. Don't let anyone tell you differently.

In January 2013, I created my Wattpad profile, @imaginator1D, for the sole purpose of reading fanfiction, specifically One Direction fanfiction. I consumed hundreds of thousands of words before I felt the itch to write. I felt like I had read every story that I wanted to read on Wattpad, and I thought I should write a chapter myself.

What did I have to lose? I had zero followers, no Twitter account, and only a One Direction fan account on Instagram. It didn't matter what anyone would think, because no one would read it. Or so I thought.

So I wrote a chapter, right at that moment. Just like that. I didn't have a title yet, a cover, any idea where the story would lead me, or if I would ever even finish it. But something happened when I posted that first 800-word chapter. I felt such a rush. Ideas and thoughts about my characters and the world I was building popped into my head, consuming every inch of my brain. Until I wrote the next chapter, and the next. I couldn't stop.

I was completely addicted to the rush and the relief I felt while writing. No one was reading my words, but I didn't care. I almost didn't want anyone to because I thought for sure they weren't great. I even remember seeing one read, then two, then three on the counter on my story, and realizing they were all from me refreshing my page.

BLAST OFF

I wish I could tell you what the heck happened between then and when people started finding my story, but to this day I have no idea what the universe did. All I know is that I slowly started getting readers. By the time I had twenty or so chapters up, my Wattpad notifications were blowing up. I was getting incredible feedback and encouragement to update. I realized there was this little group of people who were just as addicted to reading my story as I was to writing it.

That little group exploded into a million reads by July 2013, and my life had already changed. I posted a chapter a day, until chapter one hundred and one wouldn't post. I panicked and wrote a ticket to Wattpad's tech support. They told me each book could have only one hundred chapters.

So I started my second book. The comments kept growing, my read count was skyrocketing, and I just kept writing, writing, writing. I couldn't do anything else. I was too happy and too curious to see what was going to unravel in my book, just like my readers were.

"FELT LIKE A DREAM"

As my stories, now called *After* and *After 2*, grew and grew, Wattpad itself contacted me. I still remember where I was sitting when I read that e-mail. I told my husband that I thought it was someone messing with me, but I decided to write back anyway. They said they wanted to talk to me about what we could do together.

I thought they were crazy. I was an inexperienced One Direction fan writing a love story about a brooding, tattooed version of Harry Styles falling in love with a know-it-all innocent girl. Yes, my story was online, but that didn't mean anyone would actually want to publish it. Or so I thought.

My life became a whirlwind. Wattpad helped me sell my film rights to a major Hollywood studio. Then I went to New York City, accompanied by Wattpad, visiting major publishing houses, listening to editors tell me why I should choose them to publish my novel. It was insane and surreal and felt like a dream.

I decided to publish the After series with an editor who was perfect for me at Simon & Schuster. Fast-forward a year, and I'm traveling all over the world, signing my best-selling novels. Since then, my husband was able to get out of the Army, I've sold millions and millions of copies, and I've written paid stories for major companies like AT&T and Paramount Pictures.

It's all because I posted that first chapter on Wattpad.

YES, THIS CAN BE YOU, TOO

I get asked the same question over and over. "How do you become successful on Wattpad?" I can't tell you how everything that has happened, happened. However, I can tell you what I've done and what I have learned along the way.

In the beginning of this journey, I knew close to nothing except that I wanted to tell this story. I didn't know where to put all the commas, or how many words made up a book, which is why my series on Wattpad has more than one million words.

Wattpad is a magical place that creates a straight-up democracy of reading and writing. If I would have sent a manuscript to an editor in a publishing house, there's no way they would have read it. Wattpad breaks down those walls. A college degree, years of querying, having an agent aren't requirements for finding success on this platform. I've witnessed how Wattpad changed the publishing industry, story by story.

TIPS

When I joined Wattpad, I had no idea what I was doing, but I learned a few things along the way. These tips will be explored in more detail throughout this book, too.

- **PUT THE STORY FIRST**—If you are using Wattpad to write, do it with purpose. You have a story to tell and you want to tell it. Readers want to read something they can relate to, and they want to know that you love the story just as much as they do.
- **UPDATE FREQUENTLY**—Readers want you to update. There are millions of stories out there. Readers have a choice of what they can read. If you are not updating frequently, they will move on to other stories.
- **INTERACTION IS KEY**—Readers want nothing more than to know you are listening. Wattpad allows interaction through your

stories. Respect the time that your readers are giving you by commenting back. Talk with them, learn from them, listen to them.

- **TAG PROPERLY**—Readers go to Wattpad to search for something. How do they find things? Tags. Make sure that you are using the ones that describe your story (ex. romance, thriller, etc.). Don't lie to them and tag your story for something it isn't. Tag it so readers can find your story—the story they want to read.
- **DON'T WORRY ABOUT FOLLOWERS**—I can understand that you want followers. I can understand that you want to know you have a reader base. But I will be honest with you: it's the last thing you should worry about. Followers will come.
- **IGNORE NEGATIVITY**—I have been called every name in the book. At the beginning I let it get to me. I didn't understand what was happening. But what I quickly learned is that no one can take my achievements from me.

STAY TRUE TO YOURSELF

I can't reinforce this point enough. What is most important to writing on Wattpad is to write a story that you believe in.

Don't worry about what is popular.

Don't worry about what you think people will read.

Don't worry about what people will say.

My success on Wattpad is something I'm so thankful for. It's something I don't take for granted. But my success is a result of the community we have all created on Wattpad. Wattpad has changed my life.

Never lose sight of that community. Embrace it.

Good luck!

About Anna Todd

Anna Todd's After series has more than 1.5 billion reads on Wattpad. She is a *New York Times* best-selling author of *After, After We Collided,* and *After We Fell.* Her latest book is *The Spring Girls: A Modern-Day Retelling of Little Women.*

PART 1

Getting Started

CHAPTER 1

Why Wattpad Works

by Benjamin Sobieck, Editor

On Wattpad: @BenSobieck

Wattpad works because it makes it easy for readers to fall in love with your words.

I should not be writing this. When I joined Wattpad in 2015, I was skeptical. No, wait; that's not doing it justice. It was more than that. Try "suspicious." Post my stories for free? Why? What kind of scam is this?

I'd written what was some of my best work, or so I assumed, and put it up for sale using the usual self-publishing methods. Few readers cared. Even fewer picked up copies. Self-publishing, this panacea for jaded writers turned off by the typical grind, didn't work. The small presses I signed with weren't much better. The big, traditional publishers weren't answering the door. To be blunt, I was stuck, feeling hopeless and more than a little frustrated with myself, my writing, and the publishing game.

So I had every right to be cynical back in 2015. Soon after my meltdown, I read an article about a writing conference featuring a website out of Toronto called "Wattpad." The article detailed how writers post their works for free on Wattpad and then benefit from the readerships they build. Not "free*," not "free," and not even "free for a limited time." Just free. Free-free. As in, forever free, until the sun turns into a red giant and swallows the Earth or I delete the story from Wattpad, whichever comes first.

Were I not so thoroughly finished with the "normal" rules of the writing game, I would've given in to my skepticism. But at that point in time, listening to the digital crickets chirp—or maybe laugh—at the frozen response to my fiction, I had absolutely nothing to lose. I shelved my skepticism for the time being, posted a couple of works, and sat back to listen to the echo of my writer buds: "This is against the rules. You're not supposed to post your work for free." There were, of course, exceptions but none reserved for this "What-pad."

Like most rules about writing, this one was to be tossed into a meat grinder and scraped into a dog bowl. Posting those stories to Wattpad turned out to be the best decision I ever made. The reason is the same one that explains why Wattpad works. It's a simple reason, really, and brilliant. But like so many brilliant things, the apparent simplicity disguises the genius beneath. Wattpad works because it makes it easy for readers to fall in love with your words.

If you take nothing else away from this book—although I hope you take a lot more—let it be those sixteen words. Highlight them; memorize them; cut that sentence out of this book, and staple it to your forehead, whatever it takes. Because that same sense of panic and self-doubt that pushes your writing forward with questions like "How can I get better?" and "Am I good enough?" will also interrogate this decision to give your life's work away on this "Wattpad thing." And make no mistake: All writing is your life's work. The response is that same statement: Wattpad works because it makes it easy for readers to fall in love with your words.

It took me a solid year on Wattpad to learn that. I wasn't even floundering during that time. My reads on the site were going up, up, up. I understood that much, but I didn't grasp the meaning behind the metrics. What does one hundred thousand reads on a story mean to my larger writing career? Are four hundred thousand reads four times better than that? So many questions. The light bulb popped when that sixteen-word statement hit me. I wrote it down at the time, not even knowing it would end up in a book. To pull from Hemingway, it is the truest statement I can make about Wattpad, and that's why it's here.

How else can one explain the site's popularity? As of this writing, sixty-five million people visit Wattpad every month. That'd place it at number twenty-three on the list of the world's most populous countries. Wattpad didn't start out with sixty-five million users, though. The key is, again, in how Wattpad makes it easy for readers to fall in love with your words. The stories, from novels to short works to nonfiction to epic tomes, are available to read for free. It couldn't be easier to dive in. Go to Wattpad.com, or download the Wattpad app. Create a free account. Start reading. Were it any simpler, it would cease to exist in this particular corner of space-time. And speaking of laws of physics, here's one about the way people behave: They're like water. They'll pick low barriers over high barriers every time. With that in mind, sixty-five million seems low, not high.

Still, that's only part of the reason why Wattpad works. Were free content alone enough to build an online audience of readers in the tens of millions, I wouldn't be writing this. I'd be busy copy/pasting public-domain phone books to my proprietary e-reading app. Readers need writers and vice versa, so Wattpad made the experience of writing as easy as the experience of reading. If someone can type out a text on a smartphone, write a sentence on a word processing program, or compose a blog post, then writing on and publishing to Wattpad is easily within reach. Log in. Click "Create." Observe a blank screen. Type words. Hit "Publish." Done.

Of course, there's a little bit more to the process than that, as will be covered in other parts of this book, but that's the gist of it. A time-traveling Neanderthal could write several cave walls' worth of prehistory on Wattpad and not blink (if that isn't already a story on Wattpad, it needs to be). Compare this to how I and many other writers are accustomed to publishing full-length fiction in the digital era. It takes time, technical understanding, and tools to get what is traditionally thought of as an e-book live. That creates a barrier for someone lacking one or more of those necessities or the finances to make up for any deficiencies.

This isn't a theme common to the writerly zeitgeist. The advent of e-books, specifically in the area of self-publishing, was supposed to usher in a great era of democratic writing and remove many of the gatekeepers preventing a writer from publishing her work. This is true in many cases, but there is room for improvement. Trading a vertical gatekeeper (traditional agents, publishers, distributors, retailers, etc.) for several horizontal ones isn't quite what a truly democratic model would look like, at least in my mind. E-book formatting, cover creation, editing, marketing, and sales management don't fall out of the sky.

Wattpad, with its ground-up simplicity, is a step in the right direction. In addition to boiling down the act of writing to its most basic granules, it's given cover creation, editing, and marketing the same treatment. Got a simple cover? Upload it. Done. Not sure if the edits are professionally polished? Readers still appreciate raw writing. Is marketing an issue for you? Social media is baked into the platform, and readers are eager to share.

That brings to mind the third reason Wattpad works. Were reading and writing enough on their own, Wattpad would've been a product of the first century, not the twenty-first. Social media, and the sharing and community it builds, is also why Wattpad works. This is where it gets interesting. Ninety percent of Wattpad's online audience falls into the Gen Z or millennial demographic. What's a safe assumption about those demos? They're eager to share with one another on social media.

Wattpad is itself a social media network. Readers and writers can talk about chapters, specific passages, entire works, and their day-to-day lives with ease. It's like readers are all writing notes in the margins of the same print book while the author looks over everyone's shoulders. Everyone can talk to everyone else in real time. Such discussions expand the boundaries of a story's real estate in readers' heads.

This social experience is far from endemic to Wattpad. Since Wattpad doesn't ignore the rest of the digital world, other social networks are plugged into the site for quick and easy sharing, with Wattpad at the core of the web. There's plenty more to be said on that topic, and it's covered elsewhere in this book. This level of social engagement allows us to see the acts of writing and reading in a new light. No longer are these solitary ventures. Everyone in the world (or at least sixty-five million people) is on the same page, so to speak.

Combine low barriers to entry for reading and writing with social media, and the result is something greater than the sum of its parts. That difference dangling in the equation could be called the X factor, the ghost in the machine, the special sauce. Some sites have it; some don't. I could give this mysterious component another name, but it's impossible to truly define it. Why do readers and writers keep coming back to Wattpad? The secret to the site's success is best expressed by those same sixteen words: Wattpad works because it makes it easy for readers to fall in love with your words.

Wattpad's interior may be wallpapered with that phrase, but what about the digital environment outside of its ecosystem? Note the most popular digital properties and how they keep their users engaged. I won't list them here, but I'm sure their names come quickly to mind. Whatever it is that they do, they work because they make it easy for their users to [fill in the blank]. This is the epoch of digital convenience. If it isn't quick and easy, it won't exist for long because either a competitor will come up with a better way of doing things or users will lose interest. There are simply too many alternatives.

The Writer's Guide to Wattpad

I only belabor this point about ease and simplicity because it runs counter to the self-loathing and masochism of writers in general. If it isn't hard, if the writer isn't suffering, it must not be correct or worth doing, right? Though sometimes this is true, often it's all in writers' heads, along with everything else. But something must be doubly wrong if that simple, easy thing involves giving away content for free, right?

Recalling my skepticism from earlier on, the answer to that question was a resounding "Absolutely yes, something is wrong!" However, that was before that sixteen-word phrase became abundantly clear to me. There is, in fact, nothing wrong with giving content away for free. It's been done before, and it's being done right now, albeit in a different way. Wattpad doesn't work without free content.

Let's not confuse "free" with what it isn't, though. "Free" reflects price, not value. The difference is that "price" is what a person pays and "value" is what a person gets, as Warren Buffett might say. That's something that the Wattpad experience understands better than any other player in this social-reading experiment, and it's another reason why Wattpad works.

Simply put, there is value in a reader paying attention to a story or a writer. It might not be measurable in strict monetary terms, but there is definitely a transaction occurring. A writer puts out work and receives two or two hundred or two million people's attention in return. A reader devotes two minutes or twenty minutes or two hours of attention in exchange for entertainment. That this is wrapped up in a medium like Wattpad is innovative, but it's nothing new. Broadcast media built an entire industry on this model, and radio and TV are still "free" to this day. Whether through ads, branded content, or up sells, the value is monetized, but it's not for the sake of price.

What does this mean to writers on Wattpad? How can that value be exchanged for something that helps a career? That's what this guide intends to dissect. By the time you're finished with it, you'll be in a much better spot to understand this burgeoning publishing model and how it complements, not competes with, the rest of the publishing and entertainment industry. The short version is, once again, those sixteen words: Wattpad works because it makes it easy for readers to fall in love with your words.

That brings me back to my own experiences on Wattpad. Why Wattpad works is also why my work works on Wattpad (try saying that three times fast). What was missing was a corps of readers who would follow me and my writing with passion. Without that, I was wordsmithing into the wind. This speaks to the standard advice many writers hear in guides, online, and at conferences: Writers "need a platform" and they should "go build one" before doing anything else, as if readers were nails in a house. Go get your hammer, dear writer, and pound.

Maybe I'm just dense, but I missed the part that's supposed to come after that, where the creation of a platform is detailed in "do X and get Y" terms. Sure, there aren't any guarantees in the writing game, but nebulous assumptions about what social media, blogs, and e-newsletters can do to build a platform only go so far. That's frequently because writers cannot know exactly who is following or subscribing to a social media account, a blog, or an e-newsletter. "Where are all the readers?" is a common and exasperated question I've heard from many frustrated writers.

I'm not saying that social media, blogs, and e-newsletters can't build a platform. I'm saying there is more value in pursuing that goal somewhere that's full of readers in the first place. Nine out of ten of Wattpad's sixty-five million users are strict readers, and on average they read thirty minutes per session, according to Wattpad's statistics. The value of a single follow on Wattpad is therefore greater than one from another social media network. And why is that? Again, it's because of those sixteen words: Wattpad works because it makes it easy for readers to fall in love with your words.

With time, focus, and a little luck, my platform of readers grew faster than at any other point in my writing career. That led to branded content opportunities, publishing deals, speaking engagements, and more. Heck, what you're reading right now is only possible because of the platform I built on Wattpad. In other words, with a dedicated following, there isn't much a writer can't do.

If all of this isn't enough to convince you that Wattpad works, the remedy is to start posting to the site/app and see what happens. Use the tips and tricks in this guide to help you. What you'll find is that those sixteen words really are that one true sentence: Wattpad works because it makes it easy for readers to fall in love with your words. Feeling amorous?

About Benjamin Sobieck

Benjamin Sobieck is a Wattpad Star and 2016 Watty Award winner. He's best known on Wattpad for *Glass Eye: Confessions of a Fake Psychic Detective*, the Watty Award–winning sequel *Black Eye*, and *When the Black-Eyed Children Knock & Other Stories*. Four of his titles have appeared on Wattpad Top 100 Hot Lists, all at the same time.

CHAPTER 2

How Wattpad Works

By Kevin Fanning

On Wattpad: @kfxinfinity

Wattpad bridges the gap between the solitude of writing and the need to be everywhere at once online.

WRITING ISN'T JUST FOR LONERS ANYMORE

The best and worst thing about writing is that it's a predominantly solitary pursuit. The best parts are those times when you're alone with your ideas and everything clicks: A scene emerges from a blank page, and the world shuts off around you as you chase ideas from one chapter to the next. Sometimes we wonder if we'd be happier at home on the couch, watching Netflix, rather than stressing about a line of dialogue in a crowded coffee shop while your neighbor slurps his latte directly into your ear. But at the end of the day, there's nothing else we'd rather be doing. This is what you're meant to be doing. This is what you love.

The worst thing, on the other hand, is that writing isn't *wholly* a solitary pursuit. You won't get your book into the hands of potential readers by sitting alone in the coffee shop forever. You have to switch from writer mode to marketing-and-networking mode as you attempt to navigate the world of publishing.

This is where writing often feels the loneliest—the days you spend wandering the literary landscape in pursuit of a home for your writing. The long, sluggish slogs through agent queries or *Writer's Market*. Checking and rechecking the submission guidelines at the literary mag where you sent your piece weeks ago, thinking surely you should have heard back by now, but they've been publishing pieces that are nowhere near as good as yours. The #PitMad sessions that seem to spring up around you on Twitter like lawn sprinklers you didn't even know you were standing on. (Wait, are you on Twitter? Should you be? What is #PitMad? HELP!)

Perhaps even worse, once your writing does manage to make it out there into the world, no one seems to be reading it. After all those hours toiling on your manuscript, now you spend hours staring at Facebook and Twitter (ugh, there it is again) and maybe even Snapchat, thinking: *How do I get people to notice me and read my work?*

For some reason, having written the thing is not enough. Now you have to be as social media savvy as any teen. You have to be entertaining and charming online 24/7, in the hopes that someone will eventually click a link to read what you've written. Basically, your life is one big HOW: How do you do *all the things* it means to be a writer today, after the actual writing is done? And why does everyone else seem to be better at it than you?

YOU NEED TO GET OUT MORE

Establishing yourself as a writer, finding success as a writer, is about connecting with others and participating in a community of people who want to read and engage with your work. That's why most of us do it. We spend those hours alone with our writing, hoping that it might someday help us connect with other people.

But at the same time, the world of publishing is changing. The Internet! It's a thing. Literary journals are less important. There are stories of tumblrs, Twitter accounts, and YouTube videos being turned into books or TV shows. It used to seem fairly straight forward—you write a book, get an agent, get published, and *boom*—you're a writer. Maybe there's an intermediate stage of pitching to magazines and lit journals. If at times it seems as likely as winning the lottery, at least there's a logic, a process to it.

Now these writers are coming out of nowhere—kids, people in their twenties, people with mega book deals—with stories that started out as Harry Potter fanfiction. Successful writers are just as likely (if not *more* likely) to have cut their teeth on online forums you've never heard of as they are to have honed their talents at the Iowa Writers' Workshop. There are so many ways to be a writer and so many paths to publication and success that it somehow feels more challenging than ever to know what to do.

You can't just be a writer anymore, sitting alone in your kitchen, writing your book, waiting for agents and publishing houses to come calling. You need a social media presence and a blog, and you need to share different types of content across Facebook, Instagram, and Twitter. It can be overwhelming, to say the least.

WHERE WATTPAD COMES IN

You understand, there's only one J.K. Rowling, but is there no happy medium between J.K. Rowling and utter invisibility? You simply want readers, people who will read your writing, engage with it, and make this artistic journey you're on feel slightly less lonely. That's really what Wattpad does: It connects you with readers. It delivers your writing to an audience of engaged book lovers. The site takes the long, solitary journey of writing, editing, querying, publishing, and marketing and condenses it into a few simple button clicks. It's not a long, lonely journey after all. Your readers are already there, waiting for you.

Wattpad connects people who want their stories to be read with people who want to read stories. That's it. Open the app, and you can browse books by genre—everything from fantasy to horror to romance to paranormal to historical fiction and more. Scroll through the lists, and see what jumps out at you. Notice the covers that catch your eye; that'll be important later. Browse stories with thousands, or millions, of reads. This is a thing that can happen? The heart fills with hope. Open a book, and you'll see that the app is designed with the reader in mind. The stories are comfortable to navigate; the text is easy to read. Very quickly, reading on your phone feels completely natural and intuitive.

Posting your own story to Wattpad is almost as easy. If you've ever tried to publish a book in the Amazon Kindle store and are still experiencing PTSD as a result, relax: This is the opposite of that. All the technical stuff has been extracted and handled for you. All you do is sign up, fill out some profile information, enter your chapter title, write (or cut and paste) your chapter, and press "Publish." In minutes your story is ready to be discovered by the platform's sixty-five million users (as of this writing), who are hungry for stories just like yours.

But what truly distinguishes Wattpad from more traditional forms of publishing, whether it's compared to books, e-books, or literary journals, is the way Wattpad enables readers to engage with your work and you as an author. Readers can comment on your story and let you know what they're thinking, what emotions they're experiencing, as they journey through your story. They can post questions, compliments, and encouragement on your profile, and they can share your story with their followers, both on Wattpad and on other social media platforms.

This may initially scare some writers. *(Readers tell me their opinions of my work? And I should want to read them?)* We've been taught, after all our travels across the Internet, to NEVER. READ. THE COMMENTS. But the community on Wattpad is different from the rest of the Internet, and the people at Wattpad work diligently to keep things safe, polite, and thoughtful. These are readers and book lovers, after all: They're your people. The first time you get comments from engaged readers encouraging you to write faster and post the next chapter because they can't wait to find out what happens, it's like an incredible release of endorphins in your brain. You're hooked.

And that's you, building your fanbase. Wattpad connects you directly with readers and recommends your story to people who are likely to enjoy it. Your writing, the stuff you've been working on so hard, all alone, all those hours, finds an audience, and you start connecting with them. Your engagement gets them more excited about your work, and those readers have the tools, through Wattpad, to be advocates for you, telling their friends and social networks about your writing. Your readers become your fans, and fans are your biggest evangelists.

NERVOUS? DON'T BE.

Some writers may be hesitant to publish a book online, outside of the traditional publishing process. Does doing so mean that you're not a real writer or that you've given up on traditional publishing? Will it hurt your chances should you wish to pursue traditional publishing later? Not even remotely.

More and more publishers are looking for writers who not only have books but *audiences*. Publishers like a sure thing. They want writers who've already demonstrated that they can engage readers. More and more, the writers with passionate supporters have a better shot at traditional publication than the ones writing alone in coffee shops, with their social media on life support. There are many stories of writers who began their careers by posting their books on Wattpad and later saw those same books released by traditional publishers. For others, their success on the site has translated to opportunities in TV and movies. You'll read more about them later in this book. Doors open for Wattpad writers that might never have appeared otherwise. The world of publishing is changing because Wattpad is changing it. Wattpad provides a bridge—a bridge from stories to readers and from writers to audiences. It takes you directly from the solitary idle of writing to the enthusiasm of a community of readers.

Wattpad is a place for reading and publishing, but it's also a place for finding readers and developing an audience of fans. Wherever your writing takes you, they're the ones who are going to support you, rally for you, and share about you on social media when the next big thing happens in your writing career. So let's go. You're not in this alone anymore.

About Kevin Fanning

Kevin Fanning has been publishing things on the Internet since 1998. He is the author of *Kim Kardashian: Trapped In Her Own Game* and its sequel, *Kim Kardashian: #BreakTheGame*. His story, "Taking Selfies and Overthrowing the Patriarchy with Kim Kardashian," appeared in *Imagines* (Simon & Schuster/Gallery Books, 2016). He lives in Massachusetts and can be found on Twitter at @kfan and on Wattpad at @kfxinfinity. For a complete list of his books, interviews, appearances, and other projects, visit kevinfanning.com.

CHAPTER 3

The Writing Process and Wattpad

By Neilani Alejandrino

On Wattpad: @sweetdreamer33

Writing for Wattpad requires anticipating how readers experience stories on the platform.

With sixty-five million users and fifty supported languages, there is as much opportunity for reads as there is competition. In order to stand out, you'll need to reconsider your writing process. Readers on Wattpad experience stories differently from other media.

SOME THINGS NEVER CHANGE

That doesn't mean you have to walk away from what already works. Writing a story involves the heart and mind of a writer. The heart imbues the story with passion and dedication to the very end, while the mind handles the ideas and vision of the story. The combination of these two empowers the writer's storytelling to clearly communicate a message to readers and create a connection. These elements are essential in order for a story to succeed on Wattpad. They just need to be adapted for the Wattpad experience.

WATTPAD IS A PLACE OF EXTREMES

For starters, the idea driving your story must be enticing in order to stand out among the four hundred million stories on Wattpad. That number is only growing larger. You may have heard this advice about standing out before when writing in other media, but it's true to the extreme when it comes to Wattpad. A story must be unfailingly captivating.

That's the approach I took with my story, *The Girl He Never Noticed*, which has earned 170 million reads as of this writing. Some readers dove into the story again and again. It made their hearts beat faster, put butterflies in their stomachs, and lit a fire in their bones. So how did I make it? It had everything to do with anticipating the way my writing would be received on Wattpad. My entire writing process had to change.

NO PANTSERS

In order for a story to be noticed on Wattpad, planning is key. Readers can quickly tell the difference between a tightly wound story and one that was thrown together overnight. There's nothing wrong, necessarily, with writing on the fly (sometimes called "pantsing") because Wattpad's tools are set up to accommodate that work method. However, if you want to produce serious work that puts up equally serious numbers, you need to plan ahead. You need to be a "plotter."

Because of this, you must first decide on the story's subject matter and genre. Browse the genres and tags on Wattpad to determine what you will be writing about because those will form your targets. Choose something you're passionate about and a genre you're comfortable in, but let Wattpad point you in the general direction. Doing so will keep you from meandering and will help you avoid upsetting and confusing the readers once the story is live on Wattpad.

In my case, I write feel-good romantic comedies, with sexy, ruthless, and passionate heroes that make toes curl. It's like a modern fairy tale. I love writing these types of stories, and my readers pick up on that. For those reasons, I placed *The Girl He Never Noticed* in the romance genre and gave it the tags "assistant," "beautiful," "billionaire," "boss," "ceo," "funny," "hot," "humor," "love," "mystery," "nerd," and a few others. This wasn't by accident. Having that in mind ahead of time informed the entire writing process.

A NOVEL OR SOMETHING ELSE?

Wattpad doesn't set clear parameters for what is and isn't a novel. That's up to you. The scope of the story, reflected in the word count, depends on how passionate and committed you are to the story. If the story involves plots and subplots, extended time frames, and more characters, then it's best to go all in with a full-length novel of 70,000 to 90,000 words. Aside from their ability to garner more reads and votes due to the large numbers of chapters (which can help your rankings), novels offer multiple opportunities to interact with readers in comment sections. In turn, their feedback motivates me to be a better writer.

That doesn't mean that short stories can't be successful. If you're planning a story with a restricted time frame, few plot points, and not many character interactions, a short story (10,000 words or less) is a great alternative to a novel. Many Wattpad readers love to read short stories, too.

Again, these definitions aren't set in stone, but the point is to walk into Wattpad with a plan. If you're going to write a novel, write a novel. If you're not, don't. You're doing yourself and readers a disservice if you don't manage expectations right from the start.

DON'T LET CHARACTERS GET LOST

Whenever I have a new story, I create profiles of the protagonists to make them seem real and alive. They include physical appearance, basic stats, occupation, behavior, things they like and dislike, and others so I can keep track of idiosyncrasies and character traits. This can be especially helpful if writers decide to write and post one chapter at a time on Wattpad, which is a common thing to do. You need to be able to keep track of the characters. If you get lost, it'll be apparent to readers right away.

KNOW WHAT WILL HAPPEN IN EACH CHAPTER

Along those same lines, a chapter outline is useful to remind you of the sequence of events. It makes the story easier to organize, enhances storylines, and prevents plot holes. Again, readers pick up on this stuff, and they have the power to point it out right away in the comments. Shouldn't you be prepared?

Additionally, outlines speed up the story writing process. That's important because readers will want a new chapter posted almost as soon as the previous one went live. This can be grating, but you should keep their Wattpad experience at the forefront at all times. After all, they're the ones who will make or break you.

Outlines also help with writer's block, which can put a story on hiatus and drive readers away. Readers always want fresh content, and they'll let you know when they're hungry. That's a good problem to have, and you can exploit it even further by planting cliff-hangers at the end of every chapter. Don't feel like a chapter needs to have a natural finish. Cut it off right before a scene's resolution, and leave readers begging for more.

This is not only an effective way to tell a story, it speaks to the larger Wattpad experience itself. Readers shift from story to story because they have plenty of options. A cliff-hanger makes your story more memorable because there's an emotional attachment to it. It only takes a moment to reread the ending of an old chapter to get caught up for the new one. Remember, Wattpad is a place of extremes. Don't picture a reader quietly turning pages by a fireplace. Picture a reader juggling ten books and a chainsaw.

However, cliff-hangers are not good all the time. Having too many can exhaust readers' patience, especially if they're executed poorly. You'll wind up causing anger, disappointment, and frustration. Where one might naturally fit, go for it. If a cliff-hanger feels forced, you're probably pushing your luck.

WHAT MAKES FOR A GOOD TITLE?

I google the titles I have in mind to find out if there are other books using them. If there aren't any, I add them to a list of options. I come up with five titles before I narrow it down to the final one. You may have a different process, but there are certain things to consider regardless: The title should match the story's theme, convey the genre, and pique readers' curiosity. There are four hundred million stories on Wattpad. Grab readers by the collar, and pull them into the story. One way to do that is to ask for opinions from readers, family, and friends about which title on your list of options they'd prefer to read and why. After that, it will be much easier to decide which title to use. Taking a poll can also guide the cover-creation process.

REPURPOSE THE SYNOPSIS

Ideally, a story's synopsis is worked out ahead of time to guide the writing process. Writers famously don't enjoy writing synopses, but in this case it's doubly helpful because there's a natural spot for it on Wattpad. I simply boil it down to 100 words or so and put it in the story-details description box. This shortened version usually involves a brief description of the protagonist's background, what the character wants and cares about, the core conflict, how the conflict started, and how the character feels about it. It also includes the consequences should the conflict fail to be resolved.

Here's a great seventy-three-word example from *Who What When Where Why Bot* by Michael Estrin (@mestrin):

> Daniel Guzman is a lazy sports reporter who invents a robot journalist to write his stories for him. Obviously, Daniel never read *Frankenstein* because if he had, he would've known that it's only a matter of time before the monster escapes the lab and wrecks the damn place. Then again, maybe the newsroom needs wrecking, and perhaps Daniel's creation, Mike Computica, is exactly the kind of technological disruption journalism has been waiting for.

No matter how you write a synopsis, always write with clarity. The shorter it is, the better. Do not provide too much information, hints, or the ending, or readers will lose interest in reading the story. Let the story unfold naturally.

LOG LINES

Log lines are similar to synopses, but they're much shorter. They're the "elevator pitch" for your story. Some writers create them before ever typing the first word of a story to use as a guide. On Wattpad, they can also be inserted into the story's description. Here's a perfect example from *Rosehead* by Ksenia Anske (@kseniaanske):

> A misunderstood and overmedicated twelve-year-old discovers a carnivorous rose garden on her grandfather's Berlin estate and must unravel the secrets behind it—before her entire family is devoured.

TAG LINES

Tag lines are an even briefer way to sum up a story. They can be worked into the cover design; found on social media, in sharable quotes (highlight a passage and click "Share"), in marketing; or used as a preamble to the larger story description. From a writing-process standpoint, they, again, keep you focused and on task. *Textrovert* by Lindsey Summers (@DoNotMicrowave), originally published as *The Cell Phone Swap* on Wattpad, uses a superb tag line: "Can you fall in ❤ with someone you've never met?"

FLEXIBILITY RULES

With planning out of the way, it's time to start writing a new story on Wattpad. You can use a laptop/desktop computer or your mobile device, whatever is more convenient for you. Just know that you're not stuck with one or the other. You could start writing on a smartphone, save the story, and then resume writing on a laptop later. Everything is tied to your Wattpad profile. This flexibility frees you up to write stories anywhere: while at the bus stop, on a train, in the coffee shop, at work during break time, or at school while waiting for the next class.

Entire stories or individual chapters can be saved in draft mode, which readers can't see, allowing you to finish up before hitting "Publish." However, don't rely exclusively on Wattpad for saving or storing your content. Back up your story elsewhere, too. Many writers follow a rule of three: one save on an off-site service (such as Wattpad or Google Drive), one save on the hard drive of the computer/device used to type the story, and one save on portable storage (such as a thumb drive). Wattpad is reliable, but you can't be too careful. You don't want to lose your work!

WRITING THE FIRST CHAPTER

Now that the story details are all set, it is time to write the first chapter. The first chapter creates the impression of your work as a writer. Therefore, you have to nail it. Write an opening chapter that grabs readers' attention. Make them fall out of their seats, gasping for breath as their jaws drop to the floor.

This is Wattpad, so write words that speak to readers' emotions. Hit them right in the guts. You can achieve that by writing words that affect you deeply as a writer. Think of your greatest fear, your pain, the traumatic experience you've dreaded talking about, your horrible nightmares and demons. If it affects you, if will surely affect your readers. All you need is the courage to tell others about it.

A RESPONSIBILITY TO READERS

But we should also remember that writing a story involves great responsibility. Writers should be aware of word choice because it can affect some readers. They can feel hurt and offended, and when they do, they have a host of tools on Wattpad to quickly tell sixty-five million other readers about it. Sensitive topics like abuse and violence, sexuality, politics, religion, tragedies, and others should be worded wisely and with due consideration. If you're not sure about the way you're writing, research your subject matter more thoroughly until you fully grasp the consequences of your words. On that note, Wattpad allows you to label a story as "Mature (17+)." Wattpad defines a mature story as containing:

- An explicit sex scene (R-rated)
- Self-harm themes or scenes (including suicide and eating disorders)
- Graphic depictions of violence

Be honest about whether your story contains mature content. Readers can report content that crosses that line.

Even if your story doesn't feature mature material, it might contain unsettling content. In those cases, give readers advanced notice. Either insert a chapter indicating that something unsettling happens next, or insert a message at the start of the same chapter as the content.

On the other hand, some content is explicitly banned from Wattpad. This type of writing could get the story or the writer booted. Such material includes the following.

- Pornographic stories
- Stories containing sexual content with persons under the age of sixteen
- Stories encouraging or promoting nonconsensual sex
- Stories intended solely for sexual role play or messaging
- Stories that encourage any other illegal sex acts, such as bestiality or necrophilia
- Revealing any personally identifying information about other people, including real names, addresses, other contact information, physical descriptions, or private photographs/videos
- The promotion of hatred on the basis of race, ethnicity, religion, disability, gender, age, or sexual orientation, or content that is intended to bully, threaten, or harass others is also strictly prohibited.
- Any content that encourages or gives instruction on self-harm will be removed. Self-harm includes suicide and eating disorders.
- Any content that advertises products or services unrelated to or not sanctioned by Wattpad is not permitted and will be removed.

These rules may or may not affect your writing process, but they're good to keep in mind before committing to your story.

"SHOW, DON'T TELL" NEVER WENT OUT OF STYLE

While it's important to elicit a reaction from readers, don't shake out every surprise all at once. Doing so will kill readers' curiosity and excitement about the story. Give out details as the story unfolds. Be patient, even if the surprise you're keeping inside can't wait to get out.

Similarly, let the characters reveal personality traits, motivations, goals, weaknesses, and strengths through action and dialogue. That old advice to "show, don't tell" still works well on something new like Wattpad. To paraphrase Anton Chekhov, don't tell me the moon is shining; show me the glint of light on broken glass.

For example, if the character is happy, show in writing how "his smile broadened when he saw her." If the character is angry, write: "He glared at her with burning, reproachful eyes." Write like you're imagining a scene in a movie. This will make it easy for readers to picture the character you're describing clearly in their minds and will provoke an emotional response. And when readers feel something, they're more likely to comment on, vote for, or share your story. That's good news for your story's Wattpad ranking, which is even better for your writing career.

BRING A SETTING TO LIFE

A setting is important, and you can bring it to life by using the five senses to describe the surroundings. This can make a story really stand apart because many writers don't use all five. Think, "the smell of grass," "the sound of birds chirping," "the fresh air on my face," and "the wind blowing through my hair" to evoke a pleasant, sunny day outside.

To help me write the setting better, I often close my eyes and imagine myself as the protagonist. I put myself in a particular time and location. It's like traveling to another dimension. I write what I imagine and feel. That way, the setting will come across as more realistic to readers. Immersing readers in this way will keep them burning through chapters. There's nothing better than hearing about readers getting lost in your words.

LETTING READERS DECIDE

While I think planning ahead is a great route to take, some writers prefer to use reader feedback to inform the story's direction. There's nothing wrong with that, and it doesn't exactly qualify as pantsing. Handing the story over to readers is a type of plan.

Some writers take a literal approach to this, and they keep things as open-ended as possible. However, that can roll off the rails quickly. A better way to keep readers engaged and the story moving ahead is to offer a set of options. Throw the question out there in a way that matches one of your own predetermined outcomes. Should the character do this, or that? Yes or no: Is it time for this character to exit the story? Where should these characters travel to next? That way, you can still hand over the plan to readers, but you'll be confident that the story will still fit within the boundaries of your vision.

A softer approach to this is to take readers' temperatures as you write. If the comments are positive, you'll know you're doing something right. If they're negative, it's time to figure out why. You're still in control, but you're getting real-time guidance.

THE END

Every story has to end. You need to anticipate how well it will end in advance, because readers want a satisfying ending. They've invested too much time and attention for it to be otherwise. The ending should resolve the protagonist's conflict. Failing that, it should give a hint about what's to come in the sequel. This is important because some readers will make a bad ending public. Even if doing so doesn't involve spoilers, it can drive away reads.

THE SECRET SAUCE

The secret to writing on Wattpad is that there is no secret, despite what some will claim. I can only say what's worked well for me. You'll find your groove, and you'll know it when you do. I credit my achievements as a Wattpad Star to hard work. I'm passionate and dedicated, and I go to bed thinking of scenes, dialogue, and endings. I wake up at four in the morning because I'm so excited to get started on my ideas. I just love writing stories. If you do too, you already have the secret inside you. Now go share it with the world.

About Neilani Alejandrino

Neilani Alejandrino is a member of the Wattpad Star program. Her career as a writer started on Wattpad when she joined in December 2012. Her first story, *My Possessive Billionaire*, was published in October 2015, followed by *The Girl He Never Noticed* in January 2016.

CHAPTER 4

Preparing Your Writing for Wattpad

By H.J. Nelson

On Wattpad: @hjnelson

Look both ways before crossing the street and before posting to Wattpad.

YOU DON'T HAVE TO RUSH

Wattpad is designed to be intuitive and user-friendly, but what might not be intuitive is making a plan for when and how to distribute your work. Once upon a time, authors waited years for publishing deals; now Wattpad lets you publish with the click of a button. But before you start publishing left and right, it may be wise to consider what it is you want to accomplish on Wattpad and the publishing plan that will help you accomplish these goals.

When I first joined Wattpad in July of 2015, I was in a position similar to that of many new Wattpad writers. I dreamed of one day becoming a published author, but I'd never shared my writing with a wider audience and wasn't confident in my writing ability. Wattpad seemed the perfect place to start, and I was as excited as I was clueless.

Fast forward two years, and I am now a Wattpad Star with more than 140 thousand followers. My first novel, *The Last She*, was one of the Top Ten Most Read Books on Wattpad for 2016, a winner in the Fiction Awards, and a Watty Award winner with over 7.5 million reads. So how did I do it?

WHAT DO YOU WANT?

First, I considered what I wanted to accomplish on Wattpad. Then I made a plan and stuck with it. I've found that success on Wattpad doesn't just fall into the laps of a few lucky writers. It comes to those who make clear goals and a decisive plan and then follow through. If you're not sure how to do this, here are some ways to define your personal writing goals and some different plans to help accomplish those goals.

Writing Goals

Whatever stage you are at on Wattpad, it's worth your time to stop and consider what it is you hope to accomplish. Having clearly defined writing goals will help you find a publishing plan that works for you and help you be more successful with that plan. Here are a few questions to ask yourself.

- Are you here primarily for feedback from a community of readers and writers?
- Are you hoping to build a platform of readers?
- Do you simply want to practice your craft and make like-minded friends within a writing community?
- Are you a published author who wishes to expand your readership to a new audience?

Decide what it is you are looking to achieve on Wattpad, and use it to guide your publishing plan.

When I began writing *The Last She*, I was revising my novel as a part of my senior thesis at the University of Wisconsin. I published my book on Wattpad because I wanted feedback from readers who were closer in age to my target young adult audience. I wanted to see if my writing was good enough to reach Wattpad's Hot List. I began with these two small but clear goals.

To my surprise, within five months of joining Wattpad, *The Last She* was at No. 3 on the science fiction Hot List with forty-five thousand reads. In nine months it had accumulated four hundred thousand reads and had begun consistently hovering around No. 1 on the Hot List.

I'd accomplished both my goals and much more than I'd dreamed, so I began to expand my goals as a writer. I dreamed of becoming a Wattpad Star, getting published, and being commissioned for paid writing opportunities through Wattpad. But I found that all of these goals started with far simpler ones and that I was able to revise as needed. Regardless of where you are on your writing journey, rest assured that it's never too late or early to change your writing goals.

Be Realistic

Another important aspect of setting goals is to choose ambitious but achievable targets. To do this, examine what you have already written, and determine the amount of time you can currently devote to writing. One of my favorite things about Wattpad is that it gives me the motivation and accountability to commit to writing one chapter a week. Writing, like any other skill, takes time and practice to perfect, so don't be afraid to challenge yourself.

At the same time, be realistic in your writing goals and the amount of time you can dedicate to writing, and allow yourself time to grow into these goals. An athlete wouldn't run the full marathon on the first day of training. Likewise, it's okay to start small and build up to your goals.

Life Happens

It's important to remember that despite your best planning, sometimes life will get in the way. When I was writing *The Last She*, I was working and a student, and I found that there were some weeks I simply didn't have the time to write a new chapter. My solution was to always be a few chapters ahead of what I was posting on Wattpad.

I also learned from my mistakes on Wattpad. Twice I tried to start second novels in different genres that I updated alongside *The Last She*, and both times I found that I could only handle one project at a time. While it's good to push yourself, it's also good to know your limits and avoid stretching yourself thin because it will show in your work. I've found that I can only sustain the passion and time commitment for writing one novel at a time. Find out what you are able to do. It's important that you don't make commitments to readers if you cannot keep them. When I committed to updating the *The Last She* every Friday, I made it a real priority in my life and very rarely missed the mark.

Find Your Bliss

Another tool for setting writing goals is to examine what energizes and inspires you when you read and write. There is no better place to find inspiration than exploring Wattpad. Investigate genres that excite and intrigue you, and when you find a book you love, consider what plan that author is using to publish his work and how effective it is. Be critical and think about what you would change to make it better. Try to get a feel for how other successful authors publish their work and navigate Wattpad. You'll find each author has her own unique style.

One of the best ways to find your own style is to specifically identify what you like and don't like in how other authors write and update. As you explore, always remember that Wattpad is first and foremost a community. Communities support and reward those who invest in and value the community. It's very easy for Wattpad members to know who is genuine versus who is selfish and not really interested in being a member of the community.

For instance, most days I receive several personal messages on Wattpad. A few are usually the word "hi" from someone I've never met, but others involve people asking me to read their books, with no context about who they are or why they've reached out to me. I don't respond to these messages. The messages I love to receive are from readers who show genuine interest in *The Last She* or in me as a writer. These are the people I always message back because I appreciate their support and enthusiasm and want to show my own investment in our collective writing community. Once you've decided what you want to accomplish with your writing, here are a few plans to achieve those goals.

POSTING YOUR ENTIRE WORK

Some traditionally published authors come to Wattpad and post their entire work all at once. This method works particularly well for authors who want to use Wattpad's immense readership as a method to draw more readers to their other works and build a larger online presence or platform. Other writers may post a completed work because they want immediate feedback on it. If you are either of these types of writers, it might make sense to post one of your works in its entirety.

SERIALIZING YOUR WORK

Perhaps the most successful driving force behind popular Wattpad novels is serialization, or releasing a new chapter on a consistent basis (often once a week). Serialization works well for those who wish to gain followers, build a platform, peak the Hot List, and attract attention with their novels. Posting a new chapter of *The Last*

She every Friday at 5 P.M. helped me gain a following of 140 thousand and earned the story many accolades. By releasing my novel piece by piece, I built tension and excitement that continually drew in new readers. Serialization also takes advantage of one of the best features of Wattpad: the fact that it is an interactive, online community accessed 90 percent of the time from a mobile device. In today's world, many readers are looking for something short and satisfying to read, which makes a chapter a week ideal.

Another benefit of serialization is that it transforms reading from an individual, solitary activity to a social experience in which readers form a habit of coming back each week and are able to interact with each other and the author. It gives readers just the right amount of new story to keep them coming back for more but doesn't overwhelm them with the prospect of reading an entire novel.

Serialization works well for those of you who might not have a whole story written but plan to write it as you go, and would like the added accountability of finishing a new chapter a week. The same could be done with a complete manuscript, too. Here are a few tips if you plan to update this way.

Choose a day and time that you know you can update consistently, as regular updates are one of the most important ways to maintain trust with your readers. If you have the luxury, inquire what days and times your readers prefer the updates. I decided to update my story every Friday at 5 P.M. because the timing worked well for me. I thought it was a time when readers would be done with work or school, and excited to see a new chapter.

However, my planning didn't take into account that Wattpad audiences often span continents. For instance, only 32 percent of my current audience lives the United States, and even less live in my time zone. This leads me to believe that my tradition of updating every Friday at 5 P.M. was actually successful due to its consistency rather than the chosen day and time. If you are consistent and the story is captivating, then readers will make a habit of returning to your story. On the other hand, if you know most of your audience comes from a specific part of the world, it might be a good idea to post when they are most active (i.e., 2 P.M. is likely better than 2 A.M.).

When you do update, make sure that your chapters are long enough to satisfy readers, but don't overdo it. I typically aim for chapters of about 2,000 words in length. Most importantly, always leave your readers with a cliff-hanger to bring them back next week.

One of the drawbacks of serialization is that it requires some foresight or a general idea of where you want the story to go. Without this, a story can very easily veer off the tracks. Many times I have found something I want to change in the story long after I have published it. Sometimes readers will forgive you for going back and changing a detail, but many will notice, and this punishes your most loyal readers, those who are following the story as you update.

The way I combat this is by remembering one fundamental truth about Wattpad that applies to all writing: Everything starts with a draft. As one of my favorite professors said, "First get it written; then get it right." It's okay to share things that need improvement. In fact, I would argue that's what Wattpad is all about. I often make notes of things I wish to change but continue with the story, knowing that I will go back and improve it later. Don't let small imperfections discourage you from continuing your story.

LET THE READERS DECIDE

If you don't have a full novel or maybe don't have the time to commit to writing every week, the beauty of Wattpad is that it embraces everyone. Write what you can, and let the readers guide you. Immediate reader feedback and interaction is something powerful and unique to Wattpad—embrace it! Sometimes, even if you don't know where the story is going, your readers do. It's perfectly fine to adjust your publishing plan as you go; just don't give your readers whiplash by changing too often.

OTHER PLANS AND CONSIDERATIONS

Wattpad isn't only for novel writers. It also features poetry, multimedia, short stories, and writing contests. Though I can't cover them all, I will say that it's important to correctly determine which categories your works fit into so that you are publishing in the right places on Wattpad. It is also important to examine and learn from other successful Wattpad authors within your own specific genre.

PARTING ADVICE

Wattpad is a diverse community that rewards and embraces those who are brave enough to share their stories. When I joined Wattpad, I never imagined I'd end up where I am now. I didn't have a road map to success. Instead, I made goals and used a plan to help accomplish them.

But even with a plan, I found that the greatest tool I possessed was a passion for writing and the driving need to share my story with the world. Wattpad gave me the outlet I needed and an immediate and accessible way to publish. The more I wrote, the more I found that the passion I poured into Wattpad would be reciprocated by an incredible online community of readers and writers.

Regardless of where you are in your writing journey, my parting advice is to not wait any longer. Whether or not you have a plan, set your story free now and learn as you go. Your book, your plan, and your writing will all grow and change with you.

About H.J. Nelson

H.J. Nelson joined Wattpad in 2015 and has since become one of the most-read science fiction writers on the site with *The Last She*. In 2017, she was contracted by General Electric to write the science fiction short story, *The Silver Falcon*. She graduated from the University of Idaho and the University of Wisconsin with degrees in wildlife biology and creative writing. She loves traveling and has backpacked through Europe, lived on a boat in the Caribbean, and rode elephants through the jungles of Laos. But no matter where she travels, the mountains of Idaho will always be home.

CHAPTER 5

Design a Great Wattpad Cover for Less Than the Price of Lunch

by Jakayla Toney

On Wattpad: @Ms_Horrendous

Wattpad readers judge stories based on covers, but you don't need to spend a fortune on design.

When you first join Wattpad and see all those fantastic covers, you probably think, *That cover must have cost hundreds of dollars* or *I need to hire a cover designer* or *It will take me ages to finish cover-designing courses.* I've been there, believing I would have to spend loads of money on a good cover, but I was wrong. With no experience in cover design and no type of real income at the time I joined Wattpad, I found a way to make my covers for free or for less than the price of lunch.

KNOW THE COVER DIMENSIONS

The Wattpad optimal book cover size is 512 pixels wide × 800 pixels tall. It can be larger than that, but keep the proportions correct. Otherwise, the book either won't fit on Wattpad or will look odd.

THE GOLDEN RULE

As you're thinking about design, there's one thing you need to keep in mind above all else: MAKE SURE THE WORDS ARE READABLE. With around 90 percent of all Wattpadders using mobile devices, it's more important than ever to think of how your covers will appear on small screens. Large font sizes are a must. If there is no way to fit in all the words, make sure the overall design is striking and memorable with a less-is-more approach (explained in the next section).

This also applies to contrast. If the background image for your cover is dark, then don't use similarly dark letters that won't stand out. If your book's cover image is too light, darken your text. You want the title and the author's name to be easy to see and read.

LESS IS MORE

Wattpad Star Alex Evansley (@nonfictionalex) summed it up perfectly when she said, "A good cover invites everyone to the party. The story is why people stay."

How do you do that? By adhering to a less-is-more mentality when approaching cover design. That means following the rules below.

- Choosing simple, bold images
- Matching the font of the words to the genre you're writing in
- Avoiding novelty fonts (they're hard to read)
- Scrapping any design element that isn't absolutely necessary

A cover needs one image, a title, and the author's name. A cover with all of that against a solid color background is better than one using three images and a funky font for the title.

CHOOSING IMAGES

Often the first step in designing a cover is choosing an image. Look for striking yet simple images that are memorable without being complex. Remember, readers have millions of choices on Wattpad. The idea is to stand out. Research what's popular in your Wattpad genre. You may notice right away that writers pulling from the same free photo sites use the same images. You can either choose something different or use similar images in different ways. Also, picking images that are originally from popular entertainment, like movie characters, diminishes your chances of being unique—and likely violates copyright laws.

FINDING FREE IMAGES

Where do I find free images for covers? is a question with a few different answers, but let's get something straight first. Don't use copyrighted images that you've randomly pulled from the Internet. On top of being illegal and unethical, it creates a huge hassle for the writer when/if she is caught—and it could sink her reputation, too. Simply put, the fact that an image is on the Internet does not necessarily make it available for anyone to use.

Use images the right way. Some will tell you there are gray areas. There aren't. If the image isn't explicitly free, ask the creator for permission or buy the image. If those aren't options, create your own image or hire someone to do it for you. Fortunately, you don't need to spend money or time to wind up with a great cover image. I recommend four free websites that offer high-quality images: Pexels.com, Canva.com, Unsplash.com, and Pixabay.com.

BUYING IMAGES

Buying an image from sites such as iStock and Shutterstock increases the chances that the image isn't as common to Wattpad. Since paid sites offer more options than free sites, the chances are better that the image will more closely match the book's theme.

iStock and Shutterstock can get expensive, but there are paid alternatives. Canva sells some images for a dollar, even though the website is free to use. Don't dismiss these low-cost images. For example, I used one for my book *Don't Text Back*:

It matched the theme of *Don't Text Back*, it's striking, and it didn't break the bank. Whether you have the same luck depends your needs, but the point is to give low-cost images their due consideration.

If you're not finding the right image, you could also ask your readers to create a cover image for you. Many Wattpadders are illustrators and photographers, and the reward of having their work featured is often enough of an incentive. Throwing a few dollars their way won't go unappreciated either.

DESIGNING THE COVER

When it comes to actually making the cover, the good news is that there are several options available online that don't require software installation. I'll focus on one in particular. Canva.com is not only easy to use and capable of turning out a professional cover, it also comes with a built-in Wattpad template. You don't need graphic design experience for this. Learning how to make book covers on Canva doesn't take long. Canva offers two-minute video tutorials on how to add text, images, shapes, and more.

Don't confuse simplicity with ineffectiveness. The first time I used Canva to make a cover, my book received many more reads, votes, and comments on Wattpad than the cover I had before. Furthermore, Wattpad's own data shows that twenty-three times more readers will check out a story with a cover versus one without. It's hard to translate that into hard data for individual, subjective cover designs, but the point is clear: Covers matter.

PUTTING TOGETHER DESIGN ELEMENTS

Let's put the design elements mentioned earlier into practice. Here's a cover I designed with Canva:

The image was originally much lighter, but I knew I needed to create contrast to make the title pop. Using Canva, I darkened the image. To make the title stand out even more, I placed black font in white boxes. It's easy to read, even if it's on a mobile device. Also, this cover sticks to the "less is more" approach with the simplicity of the layout. It has three primary elements, which are listed below.

- A single, striking image
- Easily legible font that suggests the story's genre (horror)
- Visible author name

That takes care of the basics. The characteristics listed above would've been enough for a Wattpad cover, but I added two extras. There's the sticker on the lower right and a tag line at the very top. The sticker, earned as part of a contest, acts to entice the reader, so it made the cut for the cover. I left enough blank space for a sticker in the original version. Consider doing the same when designing your covers. The tag line was completely optional, but note how it doesn't clutter the design. It's small and unassuming so that it doesn't compete with other words on the cover, like the title. If you choose to do a tag line, keep that in mind.

Here's one more cover of mine that was made with Canva:

This example would seem to violate the "less is more" approach because there are three images: two in the background and one in the foreground. However, the background images almost disappear into the design, which allows the foreground image to pop. It also helps that the background images consist of two neutral colors (black and gray) and the foreground image features three bold colors (peach, yellow, and pink). This design technique is a great way to add depth to a cover and still keep things simple.

The title is a little different, too. The name of this story is *Stay Away from Georgie*. However, the "Stay" is at the top of the cover, and "Away From Georgie" is near the bottom. This is an effective way to lay out longer titles because cramming all the words into a single line doesn't always look appealing. Another option would've been to cluster the words together across two or three stacked lines.

Decisions like these would come after nailing down the basics. Again, stick to the principles of "less is more" with a single image, the title, and your name. Once you have a rudimentary cover down, you can play around with other elements. This is a great way to build your confidence since you know you can always go back to that basic cover and use it if all else fails.

IF YOU CAN'T DECIDE ON A COVER, ASK YOUR READERS

If you're stuck deciding between different versions of covers, ask your readers to make the decision for you. Post the versions on social media, and tell your readers on Wattpad how to vote. Maximize this by randomly selecting voters to win prizes. You could also create hashtags for each cover and require your audience to use the hashtags on social media in order to vote. This not only keeps your votes organized, it also creates a viral effect on social media that could attract new readers in the process.

HIRING OUT

Professional book designers abound, but this isn't a chapter about how to spend hundreds or thousands of dollars on a cover. If you're looking to hire out design, there's only one site you need to know about: fiverr.com. Fiverr is a website where you can hire someone to perform a task—including cover creation—for a minimum of $6 ($5 to the designer and $1 to Fiverr). Look for designers with experience in your genre, and be sure to review their portfolios to see if the aesthetics are a match (that would apply to any designer, actually). When you choose a designer, let her know what the story is about. For example, if you mention that your book will be full of blood and gore, she may design the font to be red or appear bloody. Don't assume that the designer knows the right specs for Wattpad. Tell them the exact dimensions and file type you need. For Wattpad, a 512 × 800 jpeg file is perfect.

Here are some covers I created on Fiverr:

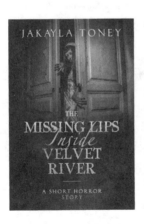

PLACEHOLDERS

If your story is already live on Wattpad but your cover isn't ready, you'll need a placeholder. This would be uploaded the same way as any other cover. The difference is that it's a super-simple design. Stick the title and your name against a solid background color. Choose "512 × 800" for your dimensions. Bingo. You have a placeholder cover.

It's better to go with a placeholder than no cover at all. Again, Wattpad's data shows that stories with covers receive twenty-three times more reads than those without. By using a placeholder, you'll reap readers and buy yourself time to finish the official cover.

THINKING AHEAD

Once you have designed your new cover, it only takes a minute to post it on Wattpad. Keep in mind that the cover can be replaced quickly if you need to do so. This is especially helpful if you turn the story that cover is attached to into a series. The books in a series should all share similar colors, fonts, and images. You could build your personal brand in this way, too. For example, I write a lot of stories involving mansions, ghosts, and wooded areas. For my covers, I frequently use ghosts and mansions. This helps new readers know what genre I write in (horror).

REVISIT YOUR COVERS

Take advantage of how easy it is to change stories' covers within Wattpad by freshening them up from time to time. Styles and personal preferences change, and there's no reason to feel stuck with a cover. You could also run experiments to see which cover design is most appealing to readers. Try one cover one week and another the next, and then examine the story's stats. Along those same lines, you might also ask readers to choose their favorite cover from a few that you're considering. Wattpad is built for this kind of feedback, so take advantage of it.

CONNECT WITH OTHER COVER CREATORS

Nearly every writer must tackle the issue of cover design, and that means you'll find plenty of support from other Wattpadders. They're perfect for bouncing around new ideas, asking for feedback, troubleshooting the cover-creation process, and providing encouragement. For a deeper dive into design, consider joining the Multimedia Designs club on Wattpad. You'll find an entire community focused solely on covers and other design projects. Find it by clicking on the "Community" tab on Wattpad and then selecting "Clubs."

About Jakayla Toney

Jakayla Toney is an American writer of young adult novels, 2016 Watty Award winner, and Wattpad Star. She is known for her horrifying and creepy ghost stories. Authors such as R.L. Stine and Mary Downing Hahn are her influences.

CHAPTER 6

Creating Usernames and Crafting a Wattpad Identity

By Katie Hart

On Wattpad: @Lilohorse

Your Wattpad username will follow you. Choose wisely.

DON'T TAKE USERNAMES LIGHTLY

Your username is the Wattpad equivalent of a first impression when you meet someone new. It can speak volumes about your work and who you are as a writer. For that reason, it's important to carefully consider the username you choose.

The usernames on Wattpad range from handles relating to a favorite band to one's own name to the name of a pet. Each name reflects the individuality and personality of the writer behind the profile. When you first begin to build your online platform as a writer, it is important that you use your username to create an online presence and unique identity. Choosing a username may not seem like a big deal, but when it comes to creating a recognizable image, it can be utilized as a valuable branding tool.

Should You Use Your Real Name?

Your username should, first and foremost, reflect who you are as a writer. Many writers use their real names as their usernames, but this decision isn't popular with everyone. It can make a writer feel exposed and uncomfortable (e.g., if he doesn't want someone he knows to stumble across his profile).

However, using your real name as your username is a potentially game-changing marketing decision. If you're a serious writer seeking publication, branding and getting your name out there is one of the first steps. Attaching your name to your Wattpad profile and any other social media accounts that you may have is a fantastic way to ensure that your name is recognizable when your books hit the shelves.

This not only helps your branding in terms of publication, but it can also help establish a relationship with your readers. Having a name to complement your picture and establishing a sense of continuity across social media profiles can minimize the distance between you and your followers, which in turn will boost your online presence.

Using Pseudonyms That Look Like Proper Names

If you're not comfortable with attaching your real name to your profile, pseudonyms are an equally valuable branding tool. They allow writers who prefer anonymity the same advantages as above, provided that the same pseudonym is used across all platforms. The brand created through a pseudonym has the potential to be just as personal as your real name and will also be recognizable on the shelves, if you carry your pseudonym with you to the publishing world. Just look at the success Charlotte Brontë had when writing as Currer Bell.

Using a Completely Made-Up "Name"

Using your real name or a pseudonym that sounds like one aren't your only options when starting your writing journey on Wattpad. Some usernames can be completely unique and not come close to looking like real names. They might combine numbers, letters, and symbols in unusual ways. There are a few advantages and disadvantages to having a completely unique username, but if used correctly, it can be a vital marketing tool.

These usernames often reflect the personality and flair of the writer, which is great for giving readers a sense of who you are before they even click on your bio. It also provokes engagement since readers will ask what the inspiration behind your username is. Unique Wattpad usernames tend to stick in readers' minds more than a writer's real name. While this isn't necessarily the best decision for a long-term venture into publication, it is a great way to garner attention. Having a less generic username allows a writer to stand out from the crowd, appear unique, and create her own brand.

Think About the Future

Failure to promote your real name means that you may have to work harder to brand yourself when you reach the publication stage. Provided that your real name or pseudonym is promoted enough on your Wattpad profile and your surrounding social media accounts, it is still possible to ensure that your name will be recognized if you venture into publishing.

Putting your real name in your bio is a fantastic start. So is connecting your real name to your username somewhere on your social media accounts. For example, both your Twitter and Wattpad usernames could be @myrealname. Then, in the Twitter bio, you could also mention that @myrealname is also your username on Wattpad and vice versa.

As an example of why thinking ahead is important, here's how my @Lilohorse username worked out. At the beginning of my writing journey, I found my unusual username really helpful. When I did a few interviews for other users' books on Wattpad, I was questioned about my username without fail. It was when I began to get these questions that I realized my screen name was more of a factor than I had thought; there were Wattpadders out there wondering what it was about. I think it made my page a lot more memorable for Wattpadders. It really did facilitate my success on Wattpad, particularly at the beginning of my writing journey. When my page became more popular, I considered changing my username to my real name, but because I'd created an image around my username, I decided against it.

However, that was in the beginning. Things changed when I went to publish my first book and I found it difficult to get people to learn my real name. I plastered my real name all over my social media and the promotion for my novel. I also had to ask my publishing company to promote the book with my username attached in order to guarantee that my fan base recognized the book as mine.

Reader Interaction

Interacting with online readers is another incredibly successful way to ensure your name sticks in their minds. Whether updating your readers, answering questions, or just putting a post out there, sign each communication with your real name to guarantee that readers know the real you. Promoting your username and real name in each post will result in readers, Wattpad partners, and (potentially) publishers correlating your username and real name.

Branding for Fandoms

Usernames can also be used to advertise specific genres. Fanfiction has become increasingly popular over the past few years, and some fanfiction stories have made their way into publication. If you're a fan of a band, celebrity, or TV show and want to write fanfiction based on your interests, having that person's/band's/show's name in your username can be incredibly useful for creating a good first impression.

For example, if you want to write about The Vamps, have social media fan accounts for the band, like to read about the band, and want to talk about them in the Wattpad clubs, having their band name in your username is a great move. If a reader has come across your work, enjoys it, and then notices that you have her favorite band's name in your username, she is more likely than not to click on your profile and explore your other works. The same goes for your social media accounts. If you advertise your Wattpad username on your celebrity-themed Instagram account, you are likely to pique the interest of those in the same fan circle and get more reads. This practice is also a great way for readers to get insight into what you write about.

A fan-based username is also a fantastic tool if you're accessing the Wattpad clubs and forums. As Wattpadders can only see your username and not your work, your username acts as a beacon that can connect you with other fans in the Wattpad community. In this case, creating your identity isn't just for the benefit of your work; it can also help establish who you are as a writer and forge friendships in smaller Wattpad communities, like fan groups.

However, like the unique usernames discussed above, there are potential disadvantages to not having your real name in the spotlight. This problem, however, is easily solved. Attaching your real name to club posts, making friends within the same fan base who are aware of your real name, and advertising your real name on your profile are just a few ways to make sure your name is accessible to Wattpadders. It doesn't always need to be on the forefront, but it does need to present. This is key in creating your online platform, your online identity, and your brand as a writer.

DON'T FORGET YOUR BIO

It is important to remember that your online identity isn't defined by your username alone. Your profile's "About Me" section is another valuable tool that can give your readers a sense of who you are and what you're about. After all, the most important part of your identity is you. When tackling your bio, it's good to find a balance between personal information and strategic information that may entice publishers and Wattpad partners. Letting your personality and individuality shine is crucial, and there are different ways of doing this without telling the world everything there is to know about you.

For the more personal element of your profile, begin with a greeting and an introduction to who you are, both as a person and as a writer. A good framework to follow involves beginning with three facts about yourself and, of course, your name. The facts that you share about yourself can be anything: what you're interested in, how old you are, what you do for fun, your favorite TV show, and so on.

This gives your followers a way to get to know you in a short amount of time and a means by which to interact with you. For example, if a follower adores the same TV show that you do, he has a reason to communicate with you. Once readers know you, you can begin to build a relationship with them, which is vital when establishing an online identity. The way you interact with readers can have an overwhelmingly positive impact on your identity as an online writer. If you're known for being open, friendly, and chatty, you'll establish a branded image that is appealing to readers, Wattpad partners, and publishers alike.

After you've decided how you want to introduce yourself to your readers, you can further flesh out your online identity. Since your "About Me" is a summary of you, it is a great space to get your creative juices flowing and show the world who you are. Wattpad readers, partners, and publishers respond well to open, friendly, and ambitious profiles, so you can use this to your advantage when building your brand.

Remember, your profile doubles as an advertisement; you're selling yourself and your works to an audience, so you can adapt your profile to suit your goals. If you're a social writer who uses Wattpad to make friends, read books, make covers, and dabble in some hobby-oriented writing, then use your profile to reflect that. Include your interests and a quote you like, and let your voice shine through your bio. If you're a fanfiction writer, talk about your fanbase in your bio. After all, your fandom will be your primary inspiration.

If you're a writer who is striving to make it in the publishing world and wants to attract the industry's attention, you can use your bio to do this, too. Talk about the genre in which you like to write, any books that you've published (if you have, provide a link), and let whomever is reading your profile know that you're serious about your writing.

Your bio shouldn't resemble a cover letter, but it should highlight your strengths as a writer while showcasing your individuality. For example, if you write humorous books, adapt a chatty tone and make your "About Me" more comical. Highlighting your individuality and personality is key, but don't overthink it—let your bio come naturally. If you're a writer who doesn't like revealing a lot of personal information on your profile, you can use this space to talk about your writing and provide a taste of your writer's voice. Everyone has one, and everyone's voice is unique, so it will shine through on your profile.

COMPLETE THE PICTURE

Your "About Me" should also include any social media accounts, blogs, and websites that you have. This ensures continuity between your accounts and gives readers a central place that they can use to access all your profiles. When you link your social media to your Wattpad profile in this way, you're also establishing a wider image for yourself. You can begin to post Wattpad-related images cohesively with any day-to-day photos that you may post on your social media. You can then begin to harmonize your accounts to enhance your identity and online presence. In blending your Wattpad identity with your social media accounts, you're broadening your reach with followers and using social media as a strategic promotional tool.

If you do choose to advertise your social media accounts on your Wattpad profile, you need to be aware that both your social media and Wattpad posts will become a huge part of your online identity. If, for example, you write teen fiction for thirteen- to fifteen-year-old girls, you need to be aware that what you post on your Wattpad page (and social media accounts) will be available to that audience. Therefore, what you post and how you interact must be carefully monitored. Each post you make and the way that you speak to your readers will have an impact on how you're viewed by others and will in turn come to shape your online identity.

PUTTING IT TOGETHER

Shaping and molding your online identity may seem like a big, intimidating task when you first join Wattpad, but it's not as complicated as it sounds. If you view your online identity as a computerized version of your real identity, it becomes a lot more manageable. View your username as a first meeting and handshake with someone new, and then view your "About Me" as the conversation you have when you first get to know someone.

Just remember that everything you do on your profile will affect the identity you have crafted. Behaving in a hostile or rude way will have just as much impact virtually as it would if you were face-to-face with someone. Be respectful, friendly, and interactive. These traits are key for building a profile that readers will want to engage with.

If you use your profile to showcase your individuality and interact with readers, your Wattpad identity will form itself. Your online brand, therefore, will shortly follow suit, but you must decide what that brand will be and how to promote yourself. Taking advantage of your username, Wattpad profile, and social media accounts is a great way to start the branding process.

About Katie Hart

Katie Hart studies literature in the UK and aspires to teach English at the college level. Her writing journey began on Wattpad in 2012, where she was discovered and subsequently published by Harlequin in 2014 and again in 2017 by Hachette Audio. When she isn't reading or writing, she is consuming the entire contents of her kitchen and compulsively alphabetizing her bookshelf.

PART 2

Crafting Your Platform

CHAPTER 7

Taking the Leap

PUBLISHING YOUR STORY

by M.C. Roman

On Wattpad: @MCRomances

Publishing a story on Wattpad isn't the end of the road.
It's the beginning.

Here is everything you need to know about publishing your story on Wattpad in order to make it a big success from start to finish.

PUBLISHING YOUR STORY

The big moment starts with hitting that "Create" button at the top of the Wattpad screen. That will take you to the "My Works" page, which lists all the stories you've published on Wattpad. Click "+New Story." The next screen that comes up is the guts of the story you want to publish.

Fill in the description (covered in chapter three), and add a cover image (chapter five). Here's what you need to know about the rest of the process.

Title

A title can serve many roles on Wattpad. First, obviously, it states the name of the story. Regardless of what comes next, that should always be the first thing entered into this field.

With that out of the way, you can add any number of qualifiers to help readers better understand what the story is all about. Remember, you only have a few seconds to "sell" your book to a potential reader.

Here are some examples of what this might look like, using a dummy title, *The Amazing Story*. Explanations are in the parentheses.

- *The Amazing Story | #wattys2017 winner* (noting an award the story won)
- *The Amazing Story | #tellyourstory* (using a hashtag as part of a writing-contest entry, a writing group, or some other initiative)
- *The Amazing Story—adventure novel* (identifying the genre and story length)
- *The Amazing Story—sequel to The Mediocre Story* (indicating it's part of a series)
- *The Amazing Story—zombies versus vampires in a skateboard competition* (including a tagline)
- *The Amazing Story [complete]* (noting the status of a story as complete since some readers like to know this before committing)
- *The Amazing Story *hiatus* (use "hiatus" when you're stepping away from an incomplete story)
- *The Amazing Story √* (inserting special characters to draw attention)

Don't go overboard with this, or you'll come across as amateurish and drive away readers. Keep it clean, concise, and enticing.

Whatever title you settle on, check whether it's being used already in Wattpad by searching for it. Duplicate titles are allowed, but it's better to avoid them, especially if the original title is popular. For example, *Chasing Red* by Isabelle Ronin (@isabelleronin) isn't the only story with that title, but it is the only one with more than 170 million reads.

Copycats will abound to poach reads, and you don't want to look like one of them. Modify your title, or add some sort of qualifier. For example, if a fantasy story is titled *The Amazing Story*, name your LGBT+ novel *The Amazing Story (LGBT+)*.

Tags

Tags are crucial in helping readers discover your story. They not only tell readers what it's about, they also appear in several locations across Wattpad, such as the home page and search results. Tags should be used as an extension of the story description so that your work reaches its target audience.

Add relevant tags that reflect your story's genres, subgenres, themes, setting, and mood. Let your readers know the most important elements of your story. Get creative, and use words that are specific to your story in order to set it apart.

For example, if your story is a teen-fiction paranormal romance set in high school that deals with friendship, self-discovery, and a whole lot of drama, make use of those keywords. In this case, relevant tags are: #teenfiction, #youngadult, #paranormal, #romance, #highschool, #friendship, #self-discovery, and #drama.

Don't forget to specify the time and place, too. This is especially important for stories outside of contemporary settings. For example, a World War II story might use #worldwar2, #worldwarii, #1940s, and #europe. Note the variations of spelling for that war. That's done to cover both of the ways a reader might type the term.

Also note that #Europe and #europe both function as the same tag. It's not necessary to use both variants. Capitalized and uncapitalized versions will work the same way.

Genre

Choose a genre that best fits your story. If your story has elements that fall into different genres, use the category that best represents it and utilize tags for the others.

> **PRO TIP**
>
> If your story is a fanfiction, whether of a known fictional character or celebrity, make sure to categorize it as such over another genre.

If your work does not tell a story or it does not fit into an established category, then it should go under "Random." Examples include contests, photo books, facts, things about me, existing song lyrics, jokes, role plays, etc. There is no limit to the types of stories you can create on Wattpad as long as they abide by the guidelines. Use your imagination, and let your ideas soar.

Language

Wattpad supports more than fifty languages. Keep in mind that Wattpad has a global audience with readers who are located all around the world and speak different languages. Make sure to select the language your story is written in so that it reaches the right audience. Wattpad is always working to support more languages, but if your story language is not yet available, you can choose "Other." Translating your story into different languages also allows you to reach new markets and an even wider audience.

Copyright

Let Wattpad know whether your work is original, adapted, or in the public domain. Do not post a story that does not belong to you without obtaining permission from the author first. Simply stating that the rights belong to another author is not enough and is considered an offense. Copyright infringement is taken very seriously at Wattpad. Any stories that violate copyright law will be removed, and your account may be deleted. On the other hand, Wattpad has a copyright support tool to help protect your work. You will have proof of creation for any story that you post on Wattpad, and it can be used for any copyright issues that arise.

Rating

Wattpad has readers of all ages, with some as young as thirteen. If your story is mature, let readers know by selecting the appropriate rating. This ensures a positive reading experience and protects readers from unwanted surprises.

Mature stories are intended for people who are seventeen and older. Rate your story as "Mature" if it contains an explicit R-rated sex scene, self-harm (such as eating disorders and suicide), or depictions of graphic violence. When in doubt, you can review Wattpad's Content Guidelines for restrictions and prohibited content. In addition to the rating system, you can also add content warnings at the beginning of your story so that readers are aware of what lies ahead.

CHAPTERS

After you enter your story's details, you'll be taken to the first chapter. If you weren't writing inside of Wattpad to begin with, you'll need to copy/paste the text of each chapter one at a time. You can do this for all chapters at once or piecemeal. In either case, you can save chapters in draft mode if you don't want readers to see everything at once.

Each chapter needs a title. Keep it simple so readers can easily navigate the story. "Chapter 1" or "Chapter 1: In the Beginning" works better than "In the Beginning." You can also use "Author's Note," "Thanks to My Readers," "Don't Forget to Read the Sequel," and other messages that fall outside of the chapter count.

GIVE IT A LOOK

Now that the story is published, see how it looks from a reader's perspective. Within the "My Works" page (get to it by clicking on "Create" at the top of the Wattpad screen) are buttons with three dots near each of your published titles. Click on those three dots, and you'll see an option to experience the story as a reader.

Does anything look out of place? Did the copy/paste introduce any errors? How are the aesthetics? Some writers make the mistake of using too few paragraphs, which results in a sea of text that's hard to read. Keep paragraphs to a few sentences.

CUSTOMIZING YOUR STORY

Once you've published your story, it's time to personalize it and make it yours. Wattpad offers several tools to enhance your story. Take advantage of these capabilities, and make your story shine.

Story-Part Features

Wattpad has some fun additional features, such as the ability to add a cast, dedicate a story part to someone, or add an external link. You can also mention other Wattpadders in the story's text by tagging them. This is a great way to give a shout-out or simply thank a particular reader for their comments. Writing does not have to be a solitary process. Get your readers involved, and let them know that you appreciate them.

Adding Media

Bring your story to life by adding visual aids! Wattpad allows you to add pictures and YouTube videos (Wattpad only accepts YouTube videos, as of this writing), either in the header of a story part or as in-line media in the text. Get creative, and customize your works with story aesthetics, mood boards, playlists, and anything else you can think of. Fueling readers' imaginations with additional material is a great way to keep them engaged. Wattpad also makes it very simple to remove and add media as you please in case you ever need to update anything.

Draft Mode

We all know stories are not perfect. Most authors need several rounds of edits to get them right. With this in mind, Wattpad offers the option to unpublish a story part. This will make it invisible if you no longer wish for readers to see it or if you want to make significant changes and republish it afterwards.

This is preferable to deleting a story part because those cannot be restored if you change your mind. You can also edit or re order your story parts at any time, whether they are drafts or published parts. Reordering story parts is very useful in cases where you want to change your story or add a new part to a story you have already written. Lastly, take advantage of the "Preview" button before publishing a story part to see how it will look to readers because this ensures that the published version is exactly how you want it to appear.

Private Stories

Once you publish a story part, it will be made public. However, you can make a story part private if you would only like to share it with your followers. Some writers like to use this feature for mature scenes or to provide bonus material for devoted followers. If you want your entire story to be private, you will need to make each individual part private.

PRO TIP

Once you make a story part private, you will not be able to make it public again. If you want to make the part public, you must create a new story part instead. Plan ahead, and use this feature wisely.

Story Status

Completing a story is a significant achievement. It is a tremendous feat that not many people are able to accomplish. Before you head out to celebrate, mark your finished story as "Complete" to let readers know it has ended. Stories designated as "Complete" attract four times as many readers as in-progress works, according to Wattpad HQ stats. Many people prefer completed works and may use search filters to show only completed content, so let them know yours is available to binge read.

SHARING YOUR STORY

Spread the word! It's often said that promoting your story is as important as writing it. Fortunately, Wattpad is a social website and makes it easy for those who do not particularly excel at self-promotion. Here are some simple ways to share your story on Wattpad.

Share Buttons

Share your story with your followers on Wattpad, promote it across various platforms on social media, or embed it on your blog or other websites. There are multiple share buttons on both the story-description page and within a story part, making it easy to share your story with just a few clicks. Wattpad will automatically generate a link to your story for you. Customize your message with an interesting line or snippet from a chapter to draw in readers. Don't forget to use relevant hashtags to cast a wider net for readers outside of your following.

Broadcasting messages on your Wattpad profile is a great way to directly reach your readers with updates or news on your stories. Make sure to click on the "Notify My Followers" box so they will receive your message.

Quote Art

Turn your favorite story quotes into art. Simply highlight a sentence or paragraph from your story, and use the "Share as a Quote" function. Choose a background image from Wattpad, or upload your own, then share it wherever you like. Wattpad will include your story title and username in the image to make it easier for those outside of Wattpad to find your story. Wattpad also has a dedicated Quote Art page on Pinterest that you can use for inspiration. It's a reader favorite!

Leverage Your Story

Your stories are your biggest asset, so use them to promote your work. At the end of your story, add a few lines to let your readers know of your other works. In many cases, people will read one of your stories but will not necessarily follow you. Unless you inform them in the story itself, they might not find out about your other books. While you have their attention, use the opportunity to plug those stories. Include the title, cover, and description of additional works, as well as a sneak peak or excerpt to entice them further. This is especially useful for stories that are part of a series. You can also tag your username in the text of a story part so that readers are easily directed to your profile and can check out everything else you have to offer.

Featured List

If Wattpad staff selects you for the "Featured" list, your story will appear on the "Discover" tab and will attract a lot of new readers, as this is prime real estate. Your story doesn't need to be complete in order to be featured. Wattpad understands that stories grow as they are being written, and having people cheering you on serves as a great motivation to keep going. Stories are featured for a limited time, but it's time well spent.

Note that writers used to be able to apply to be featured, but that is no longer the case. Wattpad staff selects featured stories. However, it can't hurt your chances to follow the tips in this chapter and throughout this book. Simply put, write the best story you possibly can.

Reading Lists

Turn your story into a walking billboard on Wattpadders' profiles. Reading lists are another great way of getting your story noticed on Wattpad. Remind your readers to add your story to their public reading lists if they enjoyed it. You can also create reading lists of your own works in order to highlight or categorize them.

Don't forget to add your favorite stories from other authors, too. Writers will appreciate it and will most likely reciprocate. Many official Wattpad profiles (which would include celebrities, Wattpad Stars, businesses, verified organizations, or Wattpad staff profiles) also accept submissions to their reading lists. Each profile has different requirements, so make sure you read them carefully before submitting your story. The more profiles that have your story on their reading lists, the more likely it is that your story will be discovered.

Dos and Don'ts

While there are many ways to share your story, there are also many ways *not* to share your story. Blasting your story any which way without purpose or direction will not work in your favor. Do not promote your story on another writer's story. This is considered spam and is disrespectful to the writer's work.

In the same vein, do not post an unsolicited story on another Wattpadder's profile or send a private message to them with nothing but the link. This is the fastest way to get your message deleted or ignored. Instead, engage Wattpadders by leaving thoughtful comments on their stories and building relationships first. This will result in meaningful friendships and will benefit you more in the long run.

Be mindful of the language you use, and be kind. Always.

DON'T WORRY IF YOUR STORY ISN'T POLISHED

"Published" doesn't need to equal "perfect" on Wattpad. Readers will overlook typos and small errors since the culture on Wattpad understands that many writers work fast and/or from smartphones. Do your best wherever your can, from the basics, like spelling and grammar, to the bigger items, like plot holes.

Don't apologize for minor mistakes, and especially don't preface a chapter by begging for forgiveness. That sets up readers to watch for errors, and that's not what you want them focusing on. Self-deprecating comments, even outside of Wattpad, paint the wrong picture of you in other people's minds. Everyone makes mistakes. Focus on your errors only as long as it takes to learn from them.

It's more important to keep moving forward, engaging with readers, and honing your craft as you go.

AN INTERESTING STAT

Wattpad's data shows that only a "tiny fraction" of completed stories clock in at more than forty-thousand words. If you're one of those writers, congratulate yourself on all that hard work. You're in rare company.

CONCLUSION

Storytelling is a continuing process of discovery. It takes time to build and hone your craft. As you keep writing, you will get better, both through practice and experience. Take the time to experiment and learn Wattpad's tools so you can make the most of it and make your story stand out.

Publishing a story is no easy task, but if you believe in it and take the necessary steps to make it the best it can be, you will position yourself for success. Above all, have fun on your journey, and I hope to see you around the orange "halls" many of us call home.

About M.C. Roman

M.C. Roman is a featured author, Wattpad Ambassador, and member of the Stars program. She is a hopeless romantic who writes new adult and contemporary romance with multicultural characters. Her debut novel, *Teaching Mia*, won the Collector's Edition Watty Award and was featured on IndieReader's Insider's Next Picks. Since then, she has built a four-book series and translated her works into Spanish.

CHAPTER 8

When and Why to Change a Story

By Jordan Lynde

On Wattpad: @XxSkater2Girl16xX

You might not get it right the first time, and that's okay.

MISTAKES ON WATTPAD ARE EASY TO SPOT AND EASY TO FIX

Writing a book takes a lot of words, a lot of time, and a lot of thinking. With everything that is happening in your mind and on your screen, it's understandable that you would make a few mistakes and create a few plot holes while writing your novel.

In the past, when you wrote a book without publicizing it on a website like Wattpad, it was up to you and an editor to find these mistakes. Some errors wouldn't be caught until after the book was finished. Then you were stuck with questions. What do I do now? How much do I have to change? Did this ruin my overall plot? How can I fix this?

With Wattpad, however, the process is different. Wattpad has sixty-five million users, as of this writing, who spend more than fifteen billion minutes a month reading the stories on the site. There are literally *millions* of eyes to catch any mistakes you might make while writing your book, and they catch them right away in real time, not months after when you've already finished the book. This makes the process of editing easier and many times more effective. You owe it to yourself to take advantage of this opportunity.

PLUG THOSE PLOT HOLES

As an example, let's say that in the first chapter of your book, you mention that your main character's father is in jail. Then, in chapter seven, your main character says his father is dead.

A reader will eventually point that out. Instead of moving on, you can decide what you really meant to do with the father and fix it. Maybe at first you wanted him in jail but then later decided it added more drama if he were dead.

You might not remember writing what you did because you're taking months to write the book, but readers are taking minutes to read it. Everything is still fresh in their minds, so they can see plot holes more easily than the writer. It's like having a real-life, real-time editor every second of every day.

TEST THE WATERS AS YOU GO

Not only are readers useful for plot holes and editing, their reactions to a scene can help you gauge whether what you wrote works or not. If you come up with a crazy idea and go out on a limb, you'll be able to see how your audience reacts to it within days. Do the comments go crazy? Do the reads drop off? Maybe it was a great idea, or maybe it was terrible one.

But you don't have to wait weeks or months to find out—you'll be able to fix it before you write the next chapter. Read the comments, and check the story's statistics. Your readers will provide you the information you need to know. If it worked out great, you can move on to the next chapter. If the response was bad, go back and edit the scene; then send out a message saying that you've updated it. Not only is it new content to read, but once again you can see if the change made it better by the responses you receive.

TAKE THE MILE-HIGH VIEW

You can use this method on a larger scale after your book is finished, too. You'll be able to see what did well in your book and what could use some work by the amount of reads each chapter has.

Chapters with a low number of reads are ones that readers didn't want to reread or never saw because they had already stopped reading the book. So if you have three chapters in a row that go 47,000, 30,000, and 45,000, you can see that something about that chapter with 30,000 reads didn't entertain your audience well enough. So instead of worrying that maybe *all* parts of your book need more work, you can easily check the statistics and rework selectively.

CRITICAL STAT: "COMPLETED READS BY PART"

This brings me to a handy feature in the statistics called "Completed Reads by Part." This is the ultimate tool for gauging how well you're captivating readers. As I said before, low reads may be an indicator that the chapter wasn't the best it could be. However, maybe it was good enough for people to continue reading the book, even if many weren't compelled to reread the chapter. The "Completed Reads by Part" graph shows you, chapter by chapter, the exact percentage of readers who completed the entire chapter in one go. This is a surefire way to know what chapters made readers drop the book.

For this example, here are the statistics from my book *Hired to Love*. When I examine the statistics for "Completed Reads by Part," I can see that it's about even across the board.

Completed Reads by Part

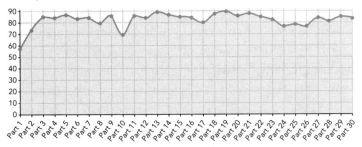

Out of the first twenty chapters, an average of 85 percent of my readers completed each chapter. However, as you can see in the screen cap, I have three major outliers—chapter one, chapter two, and chapter ten.

Chapter one and two having low completed reads makes sense because Wattpad readers generally decide by the second chapter whether they will continue the book or not. But I know something is up with chapter ten because the completed reads were consistent before and are consistent after.

So when I go back to edit *Hired to Love*, I know I need to give chapter ten some heavy loving. I'll go to the chapter and read the comments to try and discern what readers liked and disliked about it. Maybe I didn't leave an enticing cliff-hanger at the end of the chapter. Maybe the characters did something that turned off readers. Once I figure out what it might be, I can change it and see if my percentage goes up or not in the upcoming weeks.

REMOVING INSENSITIVE CONTENT

Statistics aside, I'd also like to broach the topic of sensitivity reading. Some books are criticized for being insensitive, using stereotypes, or just being flat-out offensive. Whether the author wrote something without realizing it or not, the fact of the matter is that it is in their book and it offends people.

"But how am I supposed to know what offends everyone?" you might ask.

"Well, you could do your research," I'd mumble before clearing my throat and saying loudly, "Or you can have a very vast and diverse audience read through it for you first. For *free*."

Yes, let us not forget that Wattpad readers come from all over the world. Every culture, every race, every religion, every nationality. You have more help than any sensitivity reader could give you.

If you are writing a scene and you are unsure of how to approach a topic, ask your readers. Did I do this okay? Did I offend anyone? How could I change it so that it reflects everyday life realistically? Readers have *no* trouble telling you what offends them and what needs to be fixed.

A writer can't be expected to know what offends everyone, but Wattpad makes learning easier. This way, if you release your work through a traditional publisher or self-publish, you won't displease any readers or get a bad review because you miswrote something.

CLEAR THE FILLER

And speaking of displeasing readers, Wattpad helps keep your readers happy when you take the plunge into publishing your work outside of Wattpad. When the time comes, you'll need to figure out what you wrote just for the readers, just for the updates, and what you wrote for the actual plot. There's nothing wrong with writing a lot, but filler is not important to the plot and is just extra pages to print out when the book is ready to be published. So you'll probably need to cut some.

Let's say that you need to cut thousands of words from your manuscript. You're not sure where to start, and you don't want to cut anything that will upset your readers. Since readers are so vocal, you're going to know what they love about your book and whom they love in your book.

If you go through all the scenes, you'll find that the ones readers are fond of have the highest number of comments. So, if you're
thinking about cutting a character, first see what the reader's response was to her. Did they care about that character at all? No?
Then you can cut her. If there's a whole chapter that really isn't
needed and it doesn't seem like anyone is interested in it, that
makes it easier to cut it.

KNOW WHEN IT'S TIME TO STOP

What happens when you just can't write anymore? I'm not talking
writer's block or being lazy, but when you hit that point where just
thinking about your novel is stressing you out. How do you know
when to stop writing? When to take a break? Or maybe just flat out
quit the book and start writing another?

If you're posting it as you go, your first step could be to ask your
readers. Is your story holding their interest? Can they see this becoming one of their favorite books?

In most cases, your readers are going to urge you to keep writing it. That is one of the downsides to posting online. If you start a
book and realize you want to drop it, be prepared to deal with some
disappointed readers. But sometimes it's better to drop a book than
to stress yourself out over writing it, especially when you have readers demanding updates. Once writing becomes a chore instead of a
pleasure, it's time to take a break. If it's taking you hours and hours
just to write one paragraph, something isn't right.

How do you know the difference between just needing to take a
break and dropping the book completely? Be honest with yourself.
Do you care about the book? Maybe you love it and are striving for
perfection. This could cause you to overthink things, thereby making it hard to write. That's when you just need a break.

However, if you don't feel any passion for writing it but you
want to continue because people are reading it, you need to end it.
If you're not passionate about your book, why should anyone else

be? Writers will write a lot of books. Some will be finished, and some won't. I have twenty-two completed novels and probably ten others that I stopped writing after a chapter or two. There's nothing wrong with dropping a book. If you don't, you could be wasting time on a story you don't care about. The next book you write could be the one to hit the *New York Times* best-sellers list.

KEEP GOING

Now let's say you got through the hardest part of writing—actually finishing the book. Congratulations! You mark the story as "Complete" on Wattpad and get that little checkmark on your story description. Now what? Do you move on to your next book immediately?

My advice is *yes*. As long as there isn't a huge break in the time you finish one book and start the next, your readers will follow you to your next work. It's not a one-and-done with them. If they've read your entire book, they're not just a fan of the book; they are a fan of you. Keep them interested by continuously putting out new content. You'll probably need a break from the book you finished before you start editing it anyway.

RELY ON READERS

You know your work the best, but your readers aren't that far behind. It's okay to rely on them for help, and they are more than willing to help you out. Readers are a huge plus. Think of all the benefits I've mentioned above—people who write outside of Wattpad don't have access to that. Yes, fine-tuning one's writing was once necessarily a lonely endeavor, but things are different now.

SHOULD YOU HIRE AN EDITOR ANYWAY?

None of this means that hiring a professional editor to review your work is off the table. Readers won't complain that a story is too polished. However, Wattpad readers are also forgiving, meaning perfection isn't a requirement.

Hiring an editor is a great idea if you're ready to query traditional publishers, agents, or other partners. Whether you substitute the original story on Wattpad with the edited one (by manually replacing chapter content) is a call that only you can make. You may lose valuable in-line comments in the process or turn off certain members of your audience with a sudden change of direction if they are in the middle of reading the story.

> **PRO TIP**
>
> Find reader engagement statistics by going into Create, then Stats next to your story's title. Total reads, votes, and comments for each chapter are available within the chapters themselves.

TAKE ADVANTAGE OF WATTPAD'S POWER

You have access to millions of people who can help you realize your vision. Make use of that.

About Jordan Lynde

Jordan Lynde is a YA/NA author from western Massachusetts. When she's not writing, you can find her eating at new places, interacting with her readers on social media, or watching K-dramas with her cats. Follow her on Twitter at @jordanlynde_.

CHAPTER 9

Interacting with Readers

YOUR OTHER JOB AS A WRITER

By Lauren Palphreyman

On Wattpad: @LEPalphreyman

Readers don't just come to Wattpad to read. They want to be a part of a story's bigger picture.

READERS WANT MORE THAN READING

Wattpad readers love to talk! They love to talk to each other, they love to talk to writers, and they love to express their opinions (good and bad!). Wattpad, as much as it is a reading/writing platform, is a social experience. As writers we can take advantage of this. We can use the social elements to shape and edit our stories, to build our author brands, and to grow our audiences.

Within the pages of my most popular Wattpad book, there are more than half a million reader-generated comments. Some of the comments are directly addressed to me, such as those from people who want to know when the story's next installment will be posted.

However, other comments involve readers talking amongst themselves, interacting with the story, offering positive or negative feedback, or giving detailed reviews. All are valuable to me as a writer.

In this chapter I'm going to talk about working feedback and reader reactions into the storyline, making readers feel included in the writing process, dealing with trolls, taming flame wars in the comments, and generally building your author brand through these interactions.

THE TWO KINDS OF FEEDBACK

A valuable tool for writers is that Wattpadders can interact with one another while reading and telling stories. They can private message each other, comment on profile pages, leave comments at the end of a chapter, and comment on each individual line of a story. These interactions can give writers a lot of granular insights that can be used in both the writing and the editing stages of a project. There are two main forms of feedback that a writer can receive on Wattpad: passive feedback and direct feedback.

Passive Feedback

In the same way that watching television with a group of friends can be a social experience, writing is a social experience on Wattpad because it allows readers to engage with the story and the author through in-line commenting. Readers can literally chat about the plot as it unfolds before them; they can comment on any line of text or on major story developments, and interact with other readers' comments to create long discussions.

Direct Feedback

Readers can also directly talk to an author and let them know exactly what they think, not only through commenting but also through private messaging.

WORK FEEDBACK INTO A STORYLINE

There are numerous ways that feedback can help Wattpad writers.

Measure Reactions

Whether it's a plot twist, a witty piece of dialogue, or a cliff-hanger, we can gauge the moments we've provoked a strong reaction from readers by the number of people who have commented on a particular line from the story. Even more useful, we can see exactly *how* readers are reacting and understand which bits of the story they're really connecting with.

Optimize What Resonates

Often readers will discuss certain characters, themes, or theories or react strongly to certain plot points. Due to the serial nature of Wattpad, a writer can choose to use this feedback to shape the story as they're writing it.

While the underlying plot of my book usually won't deviate from how I've planned it, I'll react to my readers in terms of smaller story elements. I'll often throw in a subplot, bring a favored character to the forefront, increase the tension between two characters, or generally add in something that I know will frustrate my readers based on the way they're interacting with the content. This doesn't mean giving readers everything they want. It's more a way of utilizing reader reactions to create even more engagement as the story progresses.

Identify Plot Holes and Pacing Issues

Keeping an eye on the way that readers are reacting to the story can allow you to identify plot holes. Whether readers are asking each other what's going on or voicing confusion to you directly, you'll know where to make something clearer or fix something that's not working.

You can also use comments to gauge reader interest as a whole. If readers are starting to get bored, they'll make it known, which gives you the opportunity to quicken the pace or add something that will hold their attention.

Listen to Direct Feedback and Constructive Criticism

Look for direct constructive criticism in your comments. If you're not getting any, ask for it. I will often ask for honest feedback from my readers, especially if I think something isn't quite working. If a lot of people identify something as a problem, then I'll see if there is something that can be improved. I find these in-depth, critical comments particularly helpful during the editing phases of a project.

Dealing with Trolls, Unhelpful Feedback, and General Negativity

I've talked about how feedback can be used in a positive way, but like anywhere online, trolls exist on Wattpad. From time to time, you may find yourself face-to-face with some unhelpful negativity. The more reads you accumulate on the site, the more likely you are to experience this.

Before I talk about dealing with negativity on the platform, it's important to distinguish between *constructive* negative comments and *destructive* negative comments.

A constructive negative comment is helpful, specific, and something that can be built on to improve a story in all the ways I've outlined above. A destructive negative comment usually isn't particularly helpful at all.

For the purpose of this section, I'm defining a "troll" as a reader who expresses negativity in a destructive way. I've experienced three distinct levels of this behavior, and I tend to deal with each type differently.

Level 1: The Destructive Troll

DEFINITION: This is a Wattpadder who deliberately tries to cause destruction while hiding behind the anonymity of the internet and is the highest level of troll.

IDENTIFIED BY: The troll's comments are deliberately and personally targeted (either at you or other people). When looking at the troll's profile, you'll find that yours is not the only story targeted.

SOLUTION: Don't waste your time talking to people like this. Delete the offending comments immediately, and use Wattpad's mute function (which can be found on the offending person's profile). This prevents the troll from commenting on any of your works. If someone is harassing you or your readers, you can also use the "report" function to alert Wattpad HQ to the problem.

Level 2: The Passive Troll

DEFINITION: This is a Wattpadder who doesn't see you, the writer, as a real person. This troll is usually trying to get attention from other Wattpadders. The troll often doesn't expect you to read the offending comments.

IDENTIFIED BY: They offer vague opinions about your story that are expressed in a non-constructive way (e.g., "This book sucks!").

SOLUTION: Don't take it personally. Not everyone is going to like your book—this is okay! However, there are a couple ways you can address this type of negativity.

1. **TAKE PREVENTATIVE ACTION.**

Show readers from the start that you're a real person, not a robot. It's harder to make mindless, negative comments to people that you feel you have a connection with. I do this by adding author notes to my stories, giving readers personal snippets of information at the end of some of my chapters, being present in the comment sections, sharing images, introducing projects through video posts, etc. I've found this generally fosters a more positive environment because readers start to feel like they know me.

2. **ENGAGE WITH THE TONE OF THE COMMENT, NEVER THE CONTENT OF THE COMMENT.**

If you feel that you must respond to a negative comment, remember that it's not for you to argue with someone about whether your book is good or not. People are entitled to their opinions. However, I will often ask readers to express themselves in a kinder, more respectful way in the future. Quite often, in these cases, I'll receive an apology from the reader, who hadn't realized I would read the comment.

Level 3: The Unintentional Troll

DEFINITION: This troll will sometimes identify a flaw within your story or react emotionally to some aspect of it in a rude or aggressive way.

IDENTIFIED BY: Comments that are seemingly non-constructive. It concerns something specific in your story (e.g., "I'm bored now" or "This character is dumb"). It could also be an expression of anger that something hasn't gone the troll's way (e.g., "UPDATE NOW, AUTHOR" or "HOW DARE YOU LEAVE ME ON THIS CLIFF-HANGER, YOU *@~##!").

SOLUTION: Often these trolls are readers passionate about your story; they're just not expressing it in the best way. Try to see the positives.

1. **LOOK FOR ANY VALIDITY IN WHAT IS BEING SAID.** If someone says something negative about a specific element of your story, even if it doesn't seem particularly constructive, you may still be able to utilize it to improve your story. If readers say they're bored, ask them why!
2. **ASK THE READER TO COOL DOWN.** If readers are shouting at me about updates or cliff-hangers, I'll often ask them nicely to be more respectful. However, I'm also mindful that their aggressive comments usually mean they're passionate about the story.

TAMING FLAME WARS IN THE COMMENTS

As with anywhere online where opinions can be expressed, things can get heated. Sometimes readers will get into arguments within the comment sections of your book.

If an argument has originated from a hateful/abusive comment, you can report the comment—which alerts Wattpad HQ—and mute the reader.

However, fights can sometimes stem from small things, like readers disagreeing about which of your characters should get together. If something seems like it's getting out of hand, feel free to intervene. Your story is your little space on the internet, and you want to keep it positive. I'll usually tell the Wattpadders involved that I don't want this argument in my book, delete the comment thread, and then follow up with a quick private message to those involved to check that they're okay.

If anything gets nasty, Wattpad Ambassadors are accessible on the site for advice, and you can report and mute Wattpadders who are harassing others. If you're not familiar with Wattpad Ambassadors, they're a select group of Wattpad writers who volunteer to support the online community in myriad ways. That includes dealing with hostile Wattpadders. Their official profile is at @Ambassadors.

Remember: When faced with negativity, remain professional. You want to maintain a positive reputation.

BUILD YOUR BRAND

Readers care about your story, but they're also interested in you as a person. Use your interactions with others to help build and maintain your brand as an author. Do this by being authentic, professional, and positive, and by letting readers see you as a real person.

Show the Real You

This took me a while to get my head around. When I first joined the site, I thought interrupting the story to talk to readers distracted them from the reading process. I was wrong. Wattpad is social, and it's all part of the experience. Don't be afraid to put yourself out there.

For example, I like to share random snippets of my daily life from time to time. I also have authentic conversations with readers in the comments, share funny GIFs and images, and post introduction videos for new projects.

INCLUDE READERS IN YOUR WRITING PROCESS

Getting readers involved in your author journey is another great way to develop your brand and grow your audience on Wattpad because:

1. It can boost your engagement levels. If people feel they're a part of a project, they're more likely to invest their time in it.
2. When people feel like they're part of your journey, it stands to reason that they're more likely to support you as an author.
3. It's fun! Writing can be a solitary experience, so it's nice to have readers who get as excited about your achievements as you do.

Here are eight ways to involve readers in your author journey.

1. **ASK QUESTIONS:** At the end of a particularly interesting chapter, ask them what they thought of it. Find out what they liked or didn't like. Who is their favorite character? Start a dialogue. Let them know that their feedback is important to you. This can be even more important when you're first starting on Wattpad and

you don't have many readers yet. Make it easy for them interact with you by giving them something specific to respond to.

2. **LET READERS DECIDE ASPECTS OF YOUR STORY:** Struggling with a character name? Can't decide on an image for a new front cover? Ask your readers to make suggestions. A good way to empower readers to make these decisions is by running polls within your chapters. Write a list of options (scenes, book covers, character names), and ask readers to leave an in-line comment next to their favorite. Use the one with the most comments in your story. I've found this boosts engagement, and it often gets quieter readers involved, too.

3. **RESPOND TO COMMENTS:** One of the easiest ways to include readers in your process is to reply to their comments. If someone gives you some feedback, asks you a question, or tells you she liked your chapter, talk to her! Start a dialogue. Even if you only have one reader to start with, make her feel important— because she is. You build your audience one reader at a time.

4. **INCLUDE READER-CREATED CONTENT IN YOUR STORY:** Let readers know that if they send you a graphic, you'll insert it into your story and acknowledge them for it. You'd be surprised how many people are willing to get involved.

5. **AUTHOR NOTES:** Leave notes in your part dividers or at the end of chapters to let readers know how much their support means to you.

6. **CELEBRATE WATTPAD MILESTONES WITH READERS:** Has your story just hit one hundred reads? One thousand reads? Maybe one hundred thousand reads? Did you rank on a Wattpad Hot List? Celebrate achievements with your readers by sharing them at the end of your latest chapter. Add a celebratory GIF. Let them know they're invited to the party.

7. **CHAPTER DEDICATIONS:** When you publish a chapter, you can choose to dedicate it to a reader using a built-in Wattpad function. When you do this, the reader's username appears at the

top of the chapter and the reader receives a notification. This is a nice way to reward a loyal reader.

8. **GIVE YOUR READERS SOME TIME IN THE SPOTLIGHT:** Find a comment particularly funny or insightful? Give the reader a shout-out at the end of your next chapter. Know a reader is writing a book in the same genre as yours? Send out a status update recommending it to your followers. Someone sends you a fanfiction of your book? Let the rest of your readers know about it.

> **PRO TIP**
>
> You can tag Wattpadders in your chapter by typing @[username] within the content. This sends them a notification saying that you've mentioned them in your chapter.

People like to be appreciated and have their voices heard. Show that you value them by spotlighting them from time to time. I do this on a biweekly basis by including a "newsletter"-type chapter at the end of my ongoing story. Within this, I feature readers' works, fanfictions, images, and funny comments. I also run silly polls about my stories and generally open a dialogue.

CONCLUSION

Social interaction is a huge part of Wattpad. It can provide valuable feedback, shape your story, grow your audience, and build your author brand. While people use Wattpad to read and write stories, they're also using it as a place to socialize. Take advantage of this. Interact with readers, include them in your author journey, and let them know they're important. They are!

About Lauren Palphreyman

Lauren Palphreyman is an author based in London. She is best known for her supernatural teen romance series, *Cupid's Match*, which has accumulated more than 40 million reads online, is published as an audiobook with Hachette, and has been developed into a pilot episode for CW Seed. She is part of Wattpad's social influencer program, the Wattpad Stars, where she has written for brand campaigns, and spoken on a panel at London WattCon. One of her latest titles, *Thorn*, has accumulated more than half a million reads on Wattpad to date. She is currently secretly plotting for Cupid world domination!

CHAPTER 10

Turbocharge Storytelling with Multimedia

by Jenny Rosen

On Wattpad: @jr0127

Create an experience, not just a story.

THINK BEYOND ONLY WORDS

What do you call a book that reads like a bestseller, sounds like a TV show, and looks like Instagram's and Pinterest's secret love child?

The future.

When it comes to creating the world of your story for readers on Wattpad, whether or not you choose to enhance their experience with audio, video, and graphic elements can be the difference between your book blending in with the rest or becoming a smash hit.

You might be thinking, *Sure, creating a story that looks, sounds, and feels like a Hollywood blockbuster/Wattpad sensation sounds like a dream, but how do I do it? I don't know how to cut a book trailer, Photoshop gives me anxiety, and I couldn't tell you the first thing about adding audio to my story. I'm a writer, not a multi media guru.*

This point of preemptive self-doubt is exactly where our journey begins. By the end of this article, you'll understand how to transform your works on Wattpad into multidimensional, immersive experiences for both you and your readers.

With the right combination of sounds, images, and movie clips, you'll create the kind of novel that catches and sustains your readers' attention, and skyrockets to Wattpad success.

STEP 1: BUILDING YOUR MULTIMEDIA BRAND—IMAGES AND GIFS

We're all familiar with the brand-name juggernauts plastered across every billboard, magazine, and TV screen around the globe. Take Nike for example. All anyone has to do is mention the catchphrase "Just Do It," and a check mark coupled with images of sleek athletes in a black-and-white commercial come to mind.

Talk about powerful branding. Something as simple as a phrase or symbol conjures up a series of images, thoughts, and feelings that represent exactly what Nike stands for and establishes a personal meaning for its audience in less than seconds.

Let's call this the "branding effect." I'm going to teach you how to do this on Wattpad within the world of your story. But before we begin, we've got to figure out your starting point on this branding adventure.

As a Wattpad writer, you probably fit into one of three categories:

- A: Your novel is completed on Wattpad (aka "posted in full").
- B: Your novel is a work in progress. You're posting chapters on a regular or semiregular basis.
- C: Your novel is sitting in Microsoft Word or Notes or on your phone, and you're preparing to make the jump to posting it on Wattpad.

The good news is that you can start building multimedia into the brand of your story at any of these stages. All you'll need to jump-start this process is a clear idea of your story, your characters, and the way you want to present them to the online world. Then it's all about matching the multimedia to those elements, which in turn create "the brand."

Outlines Help Build Brands

Branding aside, it's important for writers, regardless of how far along they are with their works, to create a general summary, outline, and/or synopsis that captures the essence of their stories. This isn't only the first step in writing a more structured and focused book but also one of the most critical stages in developing your book's brand.

This first part of incorporating multimedia into your brand doesn't involve any media at all. It involves you jotting down what your book is about, who your characters are, what your genre is, and what audience you want it to appeal to.

Let's say you're writing teen fiction about a high school football star's struggle to balance first love with his responsibilities as an athlete. Once you've plotted the details of how his story plays out, you can move on to the fun part of building your brand—fantasizing.

Use Your Imagination

That's right, ladies and gents, let your imagination run wild.

Are you picturing one of the Hemsworth brothers as your football star or a dark, brooding Tyler Hoechlin as your story's sporty hero? Are you scrolling through Tumblr to find the right picture of your fictional high school heartthrob? If so, then you're on the right track.

Fantasizing is the first step to actualizing your book's imaginary world digitally.

What does your main character look like? How about the secondary characters? What actors could play your cast? What does the book's setting look like? Does it take place in beachy California or gritty Texas?

If a single snapshot could capture your story, what would it be? What's the visual theme of your story?

Match Images to Your Vision

This is the moment where websites like We Heart It, Pinterest, DeviantArt, and good ol' Google Images come in handy. This is where you start choosing the images and GIFs that are going to become the "Nike swoosh" of your Wattpad story. This is how you create the signature look and feel of the narrative.

Whether it's choosing your story's cast by saving pictures of your favorite actors or finding images of places, props, or other significant elements that represent your book, this is where your brand begins.

Make folders on your computer, start a Pinterest board, or post images on a bulletin board to start integrating visual representations of your story.

You are the creative director.

Be picky. Not every cast of actors looks good together; some photos might not jell with others, and some locations won't make sense. But once you narrow down the list of the ones that do, start mapping out how and where you want to plant these images in your Wattpad story.

Placing the Images

Should chapter one begin with an image of your dreamy football star that gives readers a glimpse of what he looks like, or should it begin with a photo of an empty field to establish the setting?

The Writer's Guide to Wattpad

Where and how you place your images will have a powerful impact on how the reader perceives the story, so choose wisely.

Photos can be easily added to your Wattpad story. Simply find an empty space to place your cursor, and click the photo icon that pops up on the left side of the screen. You'll be prompted to upload the image of your choice directly from your computer. Select your image or images, and they'll automatically be embedded into your story.

Create Eye-Catching Chapter Headings

For a little extra flare, you can also add images to chapter headings. You know the cool, stylized chapter titles you see in published books? Now you can make your own.

Whether you decide to use free photo-editing programs like GIMP, PhotoScape, or the Nik Collection, or professional-grade paid programs like Adobe Photoshop, you can create chapter headings by simply picking a background, finding and downloading an eye-catching font or two (via dafont.com), and superimposing the font onto your background.

To add the header image, click on the photo icon at the top of the screen while inside a chapter.

It takes only a few minutes to create a unique chapter header and an update full of images that add a visual dimension to your story. Whether you're adding pictures to a new story or going back and revamping an old story that never incorporated images, expanding your story's reach by including visual media will capture your audience's imagination in a fresh, new way.

Add YouTube Videos in the Same Way

The process I just described for images could also be applied to YouTube videos. Instead of uploading a file, you'd click on the camera icon while working inside a chapter on Wattpad and copy/paste the URL of the YouTube video you want to insert.

As of this writing, YouTube is the only video platform that can be embedded into a chapter on Wattpad.

Videos could contain music, movie or TV scenes, information that further contextualizes your story, content created by fans (sometimes users film themselves reading), or even a message from you. If you can help it, choose videos that are no more than a few minutes long. You don't want readers to get too distracted.

If the videos run long, such as a fan reading your story for an hour, consider inserting them into a dedicated chapter.

You're on Your Way

Congratulations! You've made it over the first hurdle of making your story a multimedia masterpiece. Why not take things a step further and venture into book-trailer land?

STEP 2: BUILDING YOUR BRAND VIA BOOK TRAILER

The power of a good trailer can't be understated. Many of us have sat in the movie theater, scarfing down popcorn, when suddenly the new trailer for an upcoming film appears. The music instantly grabs your attention while you gawk at the heart-stopping footage. Once the joyride is over, you're already knuckle deep in your wallet, prepared to shell out your cash to see the next installment of *The Avengers*.

That, my friends, is the beauty of an effective movie trailer. It gives an audience a taste of the characters' central conflict, it hints at the juiciest scenes in the story, and it leaves them begging for more. The question is, how do you do this for your Wattpad book?

You can attempt to create a trailer on your own, or you can seek out the help of experts on Wattpad who have the technical experience to make your vision come to life.

Should you want to seek out a trailer maker for hire, head over to the Multimedia Designs Club (MDC) on Wattpad and flag down a video editor who can make your ideas come to life. Just check out the "MDC Guidelines" thread to learn how to find the editor you're looking for.

While the MDC is a great way to scout editing talent, you may prefer to take the plunge into the world of becoming your own trailer editor. Aside from the benefits of learning a new skill set, you'll also have complete creative control over your book trailer's look.

However, before you become the Christopher Nolan of book trailers, you'll need to start off with the right editing software. Applications like Final Cut Pro X (Mac), Adobe Premiere Pro (Windows/Mac), and Avid (Windows/Mac) lead the charge when it comes to professional editing platforms. The downside is that all of these programs cost a pretty penny and require some level of experience (or time to learn the ropes) in order to operate them successfully. If you have some editing know-how, cutting together a trailer in one of the programs listed above is the right path for you. However, if you're new to the idea of editing and want to jump into an easy-to-use, free program that'll help you put together a trailer without too much hassle, read on.

For Mac users, free programs like iMovie are your best friend. iMovie makes importing clips fast and easy, and the timeline (the place where you sequence your video clips) makes editing quick and painless. There are a number of tutorials on YouTube (along with the great information that comes with iMovie) that will walk you through the process of editing and exporting your trailer to YouTube, Vimeo, and beyond. For Windows users, free programs like Lightworks and Windows Movie Maker are good alternatives for the beginning editor.

Now that you've figured out your editing interface, you'll need to download the clips you want to use from films or TV shows (unless you plan on shooting your own trailer). Websites like Clip

Converter are great for pulling clips from YouTube and downloading the footage you'll import into your editing program. Make sure to note in your finished trailer's description that you do not own the copyright to the footage you used (unless it is footage you filmed and created yourself) and to assign credit where it is due.

Wattpad book trailers are almost always made with found or borrowed footage of people's favorite actors, films, TV shows, etc., so it's important to state that you don't own such footage. In addition, never attempt to use your trailer commercially for any reason. The same is true with any images or music you incorporate into your trailer or elsewhere within the story as part of the multimedia experience. If you're not sure whether including certain content is permissible, omit it.

Moving forward, here are some editing tips to keep in mind:

- Choose the music for your trailer carefully. Music has everything to do with how your overall brand and story are perceived. For example, if your book is the newly imagined version of *Scream*, Carly Rae Jepsen's "Call Me Maybe" might not be the best choice of song for your score. Music should always serve the story and emotional effect you're going for on-screen.

- Using copyright-protected music can result in your trailer being blocked. Should you upload your trailer to YouTube (recommended), they may flag certain music used in it, and selectively or indiscriminately block the video. Use royalty-free music to score your trailer, and you'll avoid this problem once the trailer goes live. Bensound.com and YouTube's Audio Library are two great resources.

- Make sure your trailer's look and feel coincide with your story's brand. If you're writing a horror story, the trailer should not include clips from *My Big Fat Greek Wedding*, even if you want to feature one of the actors from the film. Find scenes, clips, and pictures that match the look you're envisioning.

- Once you've finished your new book trailer, head back to Wattpad. Embed the video at the top of the first chapter in the header area or in the story itself by simply adding the YouTube link. This will simultaneously drive traffic to your Wattpad story and YouTube channel.

Now that you've posted a jaw-dropping trailer, your book not only comes to life on-screen but also appeals to a larger audience. If you've used well-known actors in your trailer, your book might appeal to fans of the celebrities you've featured. Fandoms are a powerful force, and if you feature public figures with large fandoms, your trailer and book might just be shared in larger circles on and off Wattpad (example: *One Direction*).

Trailers can make or break a reader's perception of your novel, so it's critical to keep it short, sweet, and engaging all the way through. Use your trailer to summarize the best parts of your story, highlight central conflicts, and grab your audience, and you'll take your book's popularity to the next level.

STEP 3: BUILDING YOUR BRAND—AUDIO

The final step in building your story's multimedia brand is incorporating sound. Adding musical suggestions or embedding YouTube videos with music into your stories can certainly help immerse your reader in the narrative, but what about bringing your characters' voices to life?

In 2017, Wattpad partnered with Hachette Audio to turn a series of stories into audiobooks that would appeal to readers in a new way. Suddenly, select Wattpad authors' characters were voiced by Hollywood actors and professional voice actors who transformed each story experience for audiences around the globe. So how can you accomplish this in your book if you're just starting out or don't have an audiobook deal in the making?

Try recording your own audiobook! Now, having a studio complete with an awesome sound engineer and Morgan Freeman on tap would be fantastic. But realistically you don't need any of those elements to create a good audiobook.

Many Wattpad authors have used free programs like Garage-Band, Windows Media Player, or even the voice recorder on their phones to record readings of their stories. Some authors choose to narrate their stories themselves, and others ask friends, family, or voice actors on and off Wattpad (such as on ACX) to bring their characters to life.

The best way to add audiobook recordings to Wattpad is via YouTube.

Here's how to format your audiobook file for YouTube:

1. Export your audiobook recording file to iTunes, Windows Media Player, etc.
2. Import your audio file into a video-editing program of your choice.
3. Drop the audio file into the timeline.
4. Export your finished audiobook video file into a YouTube friendly format (3GP, AVI, FLV, MOV, MPEG4, MPEG-PS, WEBM and WMV).
5. Upload it to YouTube, and embed your audiobook video file into your chapters. This way, readers can listen along while reading.

PRO TIP

Adding an audiobook YouTube file to your chapter header instead of embedding it into the text will allow Wattpadders to listen and read at the same time.

Finding the right voices for your characters is an exciting process, as is learning how to make a recording clear, clean, and enjoyable for your listeners. Adding an audiobook element to your story can completely transform a reader's experience as well as solidify your book's signature imprint on Wattpad.

PROHIBITED CONTENT

Adding multimedia depth to a story is exciting, but be mindful of what Wattpad does not permit:

- Media containing full exposure of any private parts, such as genitalia, breasts, and buttocks
- Media displaying sexual intercourse or any other sexual act, regardless of whether private parts are visible
- Media displaying self-harm or suicide
- Images of people that have been posted without their consent, except for public figures and celebrities
- Any media that captures an illegal act

Don't push your luck. Readers can report inappropriate content, and you don't want your story (or your user account!) booted from Wattpad.

WRITE AN EXPERIENCE

Taking the effort to use multimedia to immerse your readers in your book will make all the difference in how engaged your audience will be and how passionate they'll become about supporting the story.

Next time you log on to Wattpad, take a look at the digital canvas you have in front of you, and explore the full potential of what you can create.

Don't just write a book. Write an experience.

About Jenny Rosen

Jenny Rosen is a YA author who has been a proud member of the Wattpad community since 2011. She's a UCLA graduate, film editor, and music enthusiast. Her novels *The Runaways*; *Cheater, Faker, Troublemaker*; and its sequel, *Find Her, Keep Her*, have amassed more than nineteen million reads on Wattpad. The first two books in the *Cheater, Faker, Troublemaker* series were published as audiobooks by Hachette in 2017 and 2018.

Her literary work has been commissioned by and incorporated into major brand and film/TV campaigns for companies like Cadbury Chocolate, Soundcloud/Android, E! Networks, USA Network, and Lionsgate Films.

CHAPTER 11

10 Secrets to Getting Reads, Votes, and Comments

By Debra Goelz

On Wattpad: @BrittanieCharmintine

Treat readers well, and they'll treat you in kind.

Getting reads, votes, and comments on your stories is critical to success on Wattpad. Not only do comments help you hone your writing, but the more reads, votes, and comments you get, the more likely it is that your story will be seen by new Wattpadders. But starting out isn't easy. Growing a dedicated, enthusiastic fan base requires dedication, perseverance, and time.

In this section, I will discuss how to maximize your chances of discovery in the Wattpad universe. Although the site has more than sixty-five million users and over four hundred million stories, as of this writing, it is possible to rise to the top. On first look, these numbers might seem overwhelming, but if you think about it, they also mean there is huge potential for you to find your audience. People are on Wattpad to read. This specificity makes the site unique among social media platforms and the perfect place for a writer to build a readership.

I joined Wattpad four years ago, knowing nothing about the site. Like everyone who signs up, my shiny new profile had zero followers, reads, votes, and comments. The first story I posted was *The Perfect Guy*—an adult science fiction short about a robotics company that uses a person's DNA to build a perfect mate. It got about two thousand reads, which was good, but when I looked around Wattpad and saw stories with millions of reads, I decided that's what I wanted. But how?

I analyzed, experimented, observed, and read other writers' advice to answer that question. Now I have over thirty thousand followers and a story that has accumulated ten million reads, close to four hundred thousand votes, and well over one hundred thousand comments.

I've condensed my findings into ten steps.

1. WRITE WELL, AND WRITE SMART

It all starts with your story, one that Wattpadders want to read and vote for, one that inspires them to comment. To understand what works for Wattpad readers, it is important to know who they are and what they love. The Wattpad readership is statistically different from the traditional literary audience. Although there is virtually every type of person on the site, in general Wattpadders skew young—90 percent are Millenials or Gen Z—and the clear majority are female. The astute author will keep this in mind when writing for Wattpad.

Like anywhere in the publishing world, stories have a better chance of success on Wattpad if they are well written, compelling, original, and reasonably free of errors. Because it is easy for Wattpadders to switch to another story, our objective is to not give them a reason to leave. That being said, there are some successful stories on Wattpad that have errors and are not technically well-written. Why is this?

Most likely it is because the author has touched something in the reader. Wattpadders will forgive technical errors if they identify with a main character whose struggles are similar to their own. Characters are avatars for readers, and if they can imagine they're fighting pirates, falling in love for the first time, or triumphing over the mean girl, you will have them hooked. Stories that engender feelings of happiness, despair, lust, romance, anger, or other powerful emotions have a greater chance of succeeding.

2. **UNDERSTAND HOW WATTPAD READERS FIND STORIES**

Having an understanding of how Wattpad readers find your stories is critical to forming successful strategies.

- **THE HOT LIST**—Readers will often refer to this list of the top one thousand stories in a genre. The idea is that if something is already popular, it is probably good. You can't put yourself on the Hot List, but by getting followers, reads, votes, and comments, you improve your chances of moving up in the rankings.
- **FEATURED STORIES**—These stories are curated by Wattpad and deemed to be of good quality. The best way to draw Wattpad's attention is to write a great story and stay active. If selected, you will usually see a surge in reads, votes, and comments during your story's Feature period.
- **RECOMMENDATIONS BY WATTPAD**—Wattpad recommends stories to readers that they might enjoy based on their reading habits. Factors such as your story's ranking, how recently it was updated, and whether it has been featured combine to determine how often your story is recommended.
- **WORD OF MOUTH**—People listen to their friends. The more someone enjoys your book, the more likely she will be to recommend it to others.

3. **HELP READERS FIND YOUR STORY**

Like many places on the internet, Wattpad is a big, bustling, constantly evolving place. But there are many ways you can increase the chances of readers finding your story.

- **TAGS**—As of this writing, you are allowed up to twenty tags per story, and I suggest you use them wisely. Readers search for stories using keywords, so the more you include, the greater the chance of discovery. Use trending tags if they apply to your story. Stories are also ranked within tags, and high rankings are displayed on your profile. This makes it important to choose relevant tags so that you have the best chance of ranking highly.
- **PICK THE RIGHT GENRE**—Many stories cross genres, meaning you have options. Choose the one whose audience you believe your story will appeal to the most. But do experiment to find the best fit. Consider that popular categories, like teen fiction, romance, fantasy, and fanfiction, are inundated, while others, like vampire, adventure, and historical fiction, are less crowded, meaning your story has less competition.
- **PROMOTION**—Promote your story on social media platforms like Twitter, Facebook, Instagram, and Snapchat. Ask your friends and family to join Wattpad to read, vote, and comment on your work.

4. **ENTICING READERS TO CLICK ON YOUR STORY**

When Wattpad recommends a story, the reader makes an almost instantaneous decision to click on it or not. Most Wattpadders read on a handheld device, which means all they see is a thumbnail of your cover, the title, and the beginning of your description. It's important to ace all of these.

- **COVER**—Your book is judged by its cover. This topic is discussed in chapter five. I mention it here because it is essential to getting that click.
- **TITLE**—The titles that work best on Wattpad are ones that are simple and describe what the story is about. *Mermaids and the Vampires Who Love Them* is obviously about mermaids and vam-

pires, and has a romance component. *Alien Invasion: A Love Story* is a romance involving an alien. Both titles convey something humorous and lighthearted, which matches the tone of my stories. Don't be generic or esoteric.

- **STORY DESCRIPTION**—This is an advertising tool meant to entice a potential reader. Don't give a long, meandering plot summary. Keep it short. Include conflict and a few specifics. Ask yourself why someone should read your story. What makes it unique? What is the hook?

5. **CHAPTER ONE MATTERS**

Let's assume you've done such a good job attracting readers with your cover, title, and story description that they click on the first chapter. Now what? Chapter one is a reader's first impression, and it is critical to get it right. Begin with a great opening sentence, one that begs a question. The reader will have no choice but to keep going to find out the answer. The writing should be excellent, active, and visceral. I recommend a short first chapter (perhaps 1,500 words) and lots of white space. People are intimidated by long chapters with huge blocks of text. Break it up. Be an invitation, not a roadblock.

6. **KEEP THEM READING**

How do you get your readers to click on the next chapter and the chapter after that?

Because most Wattpad stories are posted serially, there are gaps of time between posts. It is therefore imperative to leave the reader wanting more at the end of each chapter. This is accomplished not only by good plotting and creating characters that readers care about, but also about leaving open questions in readers' minds. End your chapters with a cliff-hanger. Something the reader will wonder about three days or a week later. Updating regularly is key if you want your readers to keep coming back. Make a schedule, and stick with it. Posting two times a week is optimal, and at least once a week is recommended. If you can't write a new post in that span of time for some reason, let your readers know. They need to believe you're reliable.

7. USING STATISTICS AND DATA

Be flexible, observant, and curious. One of the great things about Wattpad is that you can experiment to see what works. There is plenty of information out there, and you should use it. Successful stories and the statistics provided to you by Wattpad make for invaluable learning tools.

Analyze what successful stories and authors in your genre are doing. Emulate them. They are popular for a reason. Use the statistics Wattpad provides regarding engagement and demographics. For example, we can see which chapters are the most popular in terms of reads, votes, and comments. We can see what kinds of chapters result in the biggest decline in readership. It's normal for the drop-off between the first two chapters to be high—50 percent or more. But when readers stop at chapter sixteen after making a significant investment in your story, that's a problem. What might have turned them off? See chapter eight for more about this.

8. ENGAGING WITH YOUR AUDIENCE

Wattpad is a social-networking site. There is a direct correlation between authors' successes and their engagement. While this can be time-consuming, it is worth the effort.

You can engage with your Wattpad readers by responding to chapter comments; by creating author notes within chapters, on your profile, and on readers' profiles; and through private messages (PM). Public comments (as opposed to PMs) can result in exponential increases in visibility. If you comment on another person's profile, then their followers may also see your post. PMs are, however, special and more intimate and can engender loyalty.

Chapter comments not only help us improve our stories, they build relationships with readers. When I started out on Wattpad, I responded to every comment, even if the reader's feedback was only a smiley face. To increase the number of comments, be inquisitive. Start a dialogue. Answer with a question of your own. Readers appreciate it when authors take the time to answer and treat their comments with respect and gratitude. They also love seeing that they have an impact on your work. An invested reader wants you to succeed. This doesn't mean you have to change your story, but let the person know you've considered her suggestion.

Pay close attention to your notifications. At the beginning, I thanked every person who voted, commented, added my story to a reading list, or followed me. Every one! If someone voted for one chapter, I thanked them specifically for that chapter vote. The idea is that there might be other chapters the reader could vote for. After interacting with me, many would go back and vote for all the other chapters.

When I was a business student, I learned that one of the most important elements of a business letter is to *ask* for the action you want the recipient to take. I applied this concept to my stories and included a request at the end of each chapter for readers to vote if they enjoyed reading it. I explained why votes are important to Wattpad writers. I also invited readers to comment, letting them know that I appreciate every one. Ask people to follow you so that they will receive notifications when you update. And lastly, if someone is enjoying your story, feel free to ask the person to spread the word.

PRO TIP

When your story is done, mark it as "Complete." Many Wattpadders wait until a story is designated as such before reading so that they avoid disappointment if a writer cannot finish. You will get an influx of reads once you mark your story as "Complete." Do this by going to the "Story Details" section of any title listed in "My Works."

9. BE A GOOD WATTPAD CITIZEN

If you are a good Wattpad citizen, you increase your chances of getting reads, votes, and comments. Here is what I suggest: First of all, take a little time to familiarize yourself with the Wattpad Content Guidelines, which are found in the "Help" section of the website. It discusses important topics like story ratings, prohibited content, categories, copyright, and spam.

One of my basic principles, or mantras, is to always give first. Comment and vote on other people's stories. Never suggest trading votes for votes or follows for follows. Find stories on the site you love, and vote, comment, follow, etc.

Be the type of reader you would like to have. If your comments are insightful and pithy, you can be assured the author or the author's readers will take note and might even check out your work.

Get to know other writers in your genre. Promote stories you love. Dedicate chapters to writers whose work you admire or to enthusiastic readers. Never ask someone you don't have a close relationship with to read your story. The only exception to this rule would be a situation where you see a story similar to yours and feel a reader (as opposed to a writer) might enjoy yours as well. In this case, you can send a PM or post directly on the reader's profile. Never promote yourself on another author's story or profile, or ask people you don't know well to promote your story.

10. KEEP IT POSITIVE

Be someone Wattpadders want to interact with. Make your profile upbeat and interesting. Highlight parts of your personality that are likely to connect with your readers. Be polite and respectful with your readers and other writers. If you do this, people will feel welcome in your stories and be more apt to read, comment, and vote. Personally, I never give any negative criticism in public. If I have constructive feedback, I do it with a PM.

Don't disparage yourself or your work. If you don't believe in yourself, why should anyone else? Instead of apologizing for work you're not proud of, make it better. It is alright, however, to tell people a story is a first draft.

PUT IT INTO ACTION

Wattpad is a constantly growing and evolving platform with sixty-five million users who love to read. Now you know the secrets to increasing your reads, comments, votes, and followers. By adopting these suggestions, you can establish the kind of platform that will help you move forward in your writing career.

> **PRO TIP**
>
> Mention your story's reads, votes, and a favorite comment or two in query letters to agents and publishers. Take it even further and include demographic information found in your story's stats so publishers and agents can better understand your readership.

About Debra Goelz

Debra Goelz is a refugee from Hollywood, where she served for ten years as a financial executive for such companies as Universal Pictures, DeLaurentiis Entertainment Group, and The Jim Henson Company. Her performing career began and ended with her puppeteering a chicken during the closing scene in *Muppet Treasure Island*. After garnering more than ten million online reads, her award-winning YA fantasy, *Mermaids and the Vampires Who Love Them*, was published by Hachette Audio in October 2017.

CHAPTER 12

Plug into Other Social Media Platforms to Maximize Wattpad

by Rachel Meinke

On Wattpad: @knightsrachel

Get out there, and get social. Wattpad readers are everywhere. You should be, too.

Wattpad is itself a form of social media, but that doesn't mean that it 100 percent replaces all other forms of social media. In fact, if you're not complementing Wattpad with other platforms, you could be doing your readers a disservice.

A DILEMMA

As an established Wattpad author, I figured that my audience had a good sense of who I was. I interacted with them in the comments and on my message board, and I answered all of the private messages I received through my profile.

Still, I didn't realize how little my Wattpad readers knew about who I was until a few years ago. As I was answering comments on a particularly controversial chapter in my new novel, I noticed that my readers tended to think that I shared my characters' opinions and beliefs on certain topics. That's when I realized that, outside of my interactions on Wattpad, my readers didn't know the real me.

And it could be that your readers don't know you either.

It's important to expand your audience outside of your Wattpad platform. Wattpad is a great resource to grow your audience, but it's also important to utilize other social media platforms at your disposal. A large percentage of readers genuinely want to know and support you.

Here's a look at the most popular social media platforms and how to use them to support your Wattpad efforts. Before you begin, don't forget to include links to your other social media accounts on your Wattpad profile. That way, your readers know how to find you.

TWITTER

The platform that I use the most to promote my work on Wattpad is Twitter. In 280 characters, you can offer your readers short snippets of upcoming chapters, quotes from previous chapters, and teasers for unreleased works. Readers also enjoy tweets that reveal a side of my characters not found in my stories.

However, for me, Twitter is more for personal use than for business, and my readers tend to gravitate toward that approach. In today's technology-saturated environment, people like to interact and build relationships. Even if it's just a tweet checking in about your readers' day, they really appreciate it. I've found that letting my readers get to know my sense of humor, personality, and style helps them see me as a real person rather than just an entity behind a computer screen.

Creating Twitter polls is another way to involve your readers in the writing of your novel. It gives your readers a personal connection to the story since they're getting to decide a concrete part of your work. I recently did this when I was unsure of what point of view I should use for my new novel. The response was overwhelming and very helpful to my writing process. I used Twitter to connect to my Wattpad platform, and the poll helped create excitement about my unreleased novel. People were genuinely excited to see how my new book would play out through the chosen character's point of view.

I also use Twitter to reinforce my Wattpad updates. After each update, I take a quote and share it on Twitter (usually a funny one). That way, if my readers missed the Wattpad notification, they can see it on my Twitter, too. Wattpad makes sharing these quotes easy. I just highlight a passage on my smartphone, choose "share as quote," select a background, and send it all to Twitter. It looks clean, professional, and eye-catching.

Not only is Twitter a great tool with which to engage your existing Wattpad audience, it's a chance to grow your audience as well. There are several Twitter hashtags that are inclusive to the writing community, too, most of which are a direct line to people who will welcome you with open arms and advice.

One of the most popular writing tools employed through Twitter is #1linewed. This is where, every Wednesday, people tweet lines from current works in progress that are associated with a certain theme. It's a great way to put your name out there and connect with other authors.

SNAPCHAT

The other social media platform that I gravitate toward is Snapchat. With short snippets of your day posted onto your story, readers get a piece of who you are as well as what you're currently working on.

I have a segment on my Snapchat called "sock game" that shows my Snapchat viewers what pair of zany socks I've chosen to wear that day. I started this as a joke for myself, as I own multiple pairs of crazy socks. It turned into something my readers love to see, and the phenomenon is sometimes a topic in my Wattpad comments section.

But as far as my writing career goes, I use Snapchat to post quick teasers about where I'm at and what I'm working on. I often write outside of my home, so I might post a quick picture of my writing location and how inspired I'm feeling by it. If I'm working on an update that's scheduled to go up later that day or week, I'll post a couple of paragraphs solely on my Snapchat, allowing for those viewers to get a sneak peek of what's to come.

This is also a great social-media app with which to involve your readers in your daily life and introduce your personality quirks. Outside of my writing, I tend to post when I'm at family events, football games, or even the gym. My readers like having this personal level of interaction with me, as it gives them an idea of who I am in my everyday life.

INSTAGRAM

Another popular social media platform to tie into Wattpad is Instagram, a photo and video sharing app. Instagram is highly visual, so I use this platform to tease covers and banners of unreleased novels. This helps keep my readers in the loop as to what projects I'm working on outside of Wattpad and keeps them excited for my future works.

As the release date for my novel gets closer, I continue to post teaser images that I've curated. My readers will interact in the comments, discussing my new story and encouraging one another to read it. This kind of hype about a new story helps draw more readers into the first chapter.

I also use my Instagram to post about my personal life. As I've mentioned earlier in this article, readers want to know you outside of your writing life. My readers particularly like to see my accomplishments. My most-liked picture on my Instagram is my college graduation picture, about which I received an influx of love and support for taking another step toward my future. My readers genuinely enjoy feeling included in these milestones with me, and I love knowing that I have their support as I continue on my life's journey.

YOUTUBE

After I realized my readers didn't know much about me, I decided to open up by answering their questions. I had them tweet me with a specific hashtag and post questions on my Wattpad page. I gathered as many as I could and sat down to film a video. This was my readers' first proper time seeing me, outside of the tiny, circular photo I had on my Wattpad profile.

That video is still available on YouTube, with grainy image quality and poorly edited clips. I filmed it on my computer webcam and edited it on a MacBook available to me at my local college. My readers actually saw me and heard me speak for the first time, and it shocked a great deal of them. Through the comments, I learned that people had a much different vision of who I was in their head, from the way I looked to the way my voice sounded and even my belief systems.

I've done a couple of Q&A videos since then, and when I go on vacations, I'll often film some things that I edit together for a quick YouTube video. I'm not an avid user, and I don't upload frequently, but when I do, I often receive a positive response from my readers.

Beyond that, I began using the channel to talk about what books I'm currently reading, and in that way my platform helps promote other authors. This quickly became a popular series with thousands of views. While my readers enjoy my books, they like to know what other books I would recommend and why. I keep my reviews positive, as I know how much work goes into each individual book. But I also keep my reviews honest, which is what pulls my readers toward those videos. Offering my readers a slew of other books to read shows them that I'm continuing to actively improve upon my craft. I'm always reading and always taking notes from other authors, and I like to share these tips and tricks with my audience.

FACEBOOK

As a new creator on Wattpad, one of the first things I did was create a Facebook page. At the time, I created it for a single novel that I was writing, my first one to go viral on Wattpad. Now, however, I have an author page dedicated to my work as a whole.

I tend not to use Facebook as often as I used to due to its new terms that make it difficult to reach followers without paying for ads. But whenever I have a big announcement, such as a new book or project I'm working on, I'll include a link on my Facebook page.

I also use my page to post user-submitted art. I've received fan art and book covers for the novels I'm working on, and I wanted a way to showcase them. I couldn't post them all on my Instagram, as there are hundreds of pieces, so I began creating albums on my Facebook page. I sort the pictures by book, and I credit the people who created them in the post. Showcasing the work that my audience creates makes it more likely that they will continue to send me original pieces. It's truly an honor to have my characters and novels act as inspiration for other people's creations, and I want to showcase that as much as I possibly can.

OVERWHELMED

Starting your own public social media accounts and continually growing them can be a daunting task because of the time commitments. It can also be difficult to transfer audiences from one site to another, and not all of your readers will follow you on all of your social media sites.

If you're overwhelmed by the idea of expanding your platform through social media, here are a few quick tips.

- Use a consistent username. It's easier to find you that way, and people are more likely to search you in one go.
- Remind your readers. Always put a note at the end of your chapters that tells your audience what social media sites you're available on and which ones you frequent most. Be sure to include your username(s) as well.
- Don't spam. Don't simply use social media to promote your work, as people will generally lose interest. Offer tidbits about your day and funny anecdotes to help break up the self-promotion.
- Be yourself. Your readers are interested in getting to know who you are outside of the author realm. Don't be afraid to show them that you're not just a writing machine.

Take it from someone who started posting to Wattpad on a whim during a boring Monday afternoon: Anything is possible. You just have to start somewhere.

About Rachel Meinke

Rachel Meinke is a writer from the Sunshine State of Florida. She's a graduate of the University of Central Florida and is currently on her way to a masters in fine arts. In her free time, you can find her at the beach, the closest amusement park, or a used bookstore, browsing the bookshelves so she can add to her always-growing collection. She is a lover of animals and a collector of candles, and she is addicted to sappy books and movies.

CHAPTER 13

Network with Other Wattpad Writers to Build Communities

By Kelly Anne Blount

On Wattpad: @KellyAnneBlount

Teaming up with other writers on Wattpad can be a serious force multiplier.

IT'S TIME TO TEAM UP

Networking is a vital skill necessary for writers across all platforms. This holds especially true for writers on Wattpad. Teaming up with other writers on Wattpad can help build your community both on and off the platform. Networking on Wattpad can take many shapes and forms. For this chapter, I have detailed nine Wattpad networking hacks that I highly recommend to writers interested in building their communities.

PUT YOUR BEST FOOT FORWARD

It doesn't matter if you're new to Wattpad or if you've been there for years, your profile is important. Think of it as a business card. You wouldn't attend a professional networking event without nice business cards, would you?

Create a free, eye-catching banner using Canva, PicMonkey, Photoshop or any other cover-creation sites or programs that you feel comfortable using. You should also post an error-free bio with a little bit of info about yourself, your work, and the other places your fans can find you.

This is also a good time to check out other Wattpadders' profiles and find several writers to follow. You can read their work and leave comments. Voting is always appreciated as well. Note that many writers do not accept read requests. It is considered poor etiquette to ask other writers to read your work, whether through a private message, a wall comment, or a post on one of their works. Now, if you are friends and you feel comfortable asking (or if someone offers), that's fine. Just avoid pestering people you do not know with reading requests.

MAKE FRIENDS

Making friends on Wattpad is a rewarding experience that will expand your audience on and off the platform. Here's the best part: Making friends is as easy as clicking on profiles you find intriguing and leaving messages on those users' walls or sending them private messages. Remember to be kind and courteous when you are reaching out to other users. Simply sending a link to your story or demanding that someone read your story and provide feedback are gestures that are likely to be ignored. Bottom line: Treat others on Wattpad the way you would like to be treated.

How does making friends on Wattpad help you build your community off the platform? It's simple! Many of my fans and friends on Wattpad also follow me on Twitter, Instagram, Facebook, and Snapchat. To make it easy, I recommend using the same username across all platforms. To find me on any social media platform, all you need to do is search for KellyAnneBlount. You want to make it as easy as possible for your fans to find you.

In addition to building my social media platforms, I have made wonderful friends on Wattpad, many of whom I have had the chance to meet in person. From cohosting an epic gathering of Wattpadders at NYC WattCon to cohosting a writer's retreat for Wattpad authors, attending Comic-Con with Wattpad friends, and speaking at the RT Booklovers Convention, I have hung out with my Wattpad family close to a dozen times over the past two years. These are the people I call, text, or Skype when I need advice on writing, publishing, life, and everything in between. From Wattpad users to close friends, I cannot even begin to express how valuable these people are to me.

JOIN AN ANTHOLOGY

Joining an anthology is also a great networking activity. Working together with other Wattpad writers can help increase your online fanbase. I've participated in several anthologies, including a recent Jack the Ripper collection. The anthology featured Ben Sobieck and several of Wattpad's hottest horror writers. With a combined marketing effort, the anthology quickly shot up through the Hot List and gained more than seven thousand votes in a month.

How do anthologies work on Wattpad? Typically, one Wattpad user hosts them and contributing authors are tagged or given a chapter dedication to distinguish their work. The great thing is that working together can introduce your work (as well as your fellow writers') to a new group of readers. Sending out messages on Wattpad and across your other social media platforms will help increase the visibility of the anthologies in which you participate.

Anthologies can also be helpful in promoting works you are selling on other platforms. I created an anthology on Wattpad that helped promote a published work I contributed to along with fifteen other Wattpad authors. We shared the first chapter of each of our stories, our covers, and the buy links. This helped increase our overall sales.

Anthologies are often created among friends or through contests. They typically follow a theme or focus on a specific topic. Not sure where to find an anthology to participate in? Just start one yourself, and ask several of your Wattpad friends to join you.

PARTICIPATE IN AN ONLINE EVENT

An online event could be a regular gathering of writers focused on a specific purpose or theme, or it could be a one-time thing. They're different from anthologies in that they can take any number of shapes. Often the result isn't a complete work or set of works. They're typically aimed at showcasing writers' talents beyond a story.

One example, the Wattpad Block Party, holds a special place in my heart. I started this project back in 2015, and I'm continuing it in 2018 and beyond. As the host of the Wattpad Block Party, I've had the privilege of working with hundreds of Wattpad authors on a biannual basis.

How does the Wattpad Block Party work? Each author is featured for a full day during the event, which runs for an entire month (every February and August, as of this writing). On their feature day, each author shares a unique post created specifically for the Wattpad Block Party. The posts typically focus on a current work in progress, a Wattpad story, a published work, and/or a specific skillset they have related to reading or writing (i.e., instructions on how to create an enticing cover, the editing process, etc.). Readers can expect to find anything from character interviews to sneak peeks and storyboards. We also use the hashtag

#WattpadBlockParty across platforms to quickly identify featured authors and interested readers. Not only is this a great opportunity to network, Wattpad users also get their work in front of thousands of new readers. It's a wonderful way for writers to connect with Wattpadders from around the globe.

In addition to building their networks with new readers, authors often enjoy meeting one another in a private Facebook group created for the featured Wattpad Block Party writers. We frequently share the links to all of our social media pages and follow one another's accounts.

FIND BLOGGERS, CRITIQUE PARTNERS, AND BETA READERS

Wattpad is the perfect place to find people interested in reading and writing. This is what makes it an ideal platform to find bloggers, critique partners, and beta readers.

Bloggers help make the literary world go 'round, and one of the great things about Wattpad is that there are amazing bloggers on the platform. You can look for bloggers via the search bar, post a request on your board, and check out the community clubs. I have worked with several great bloggers who have helped promote my work on and off Wattpad. I am beyond appreciative to these generous people.

Critique partners are also abundant on Wattpad. You will want to be very thoughtful before entering into a critique partnership with another individual. The purpose of a critique partner can be varied. You may want someone to point out issues with the plot or look for grammar errors. Before you approach someone, take your time looking through their work or talk to them about their critiquing process. By working with critique partners, the quality of your manuscript should improve. Work with those whose skills you admire.

Wattpad is also an awesome place to search for beta readers. Much like critique partners, it may be helpful to seek a beta reader to evaluate your unpublished work or any projects you are looking to improve. Beta readers are also great people to approach about posting reviews of your work. Since new readers are more likely to purchase a book that other readers seemed to enjoy, accumulating positive reviews can be invaluable. By gathering a network of reliable beta readers, you will surely grow your community both on and off of Wattpad.

RESPOND TO FANS

Another important aspect of networking on Wattpad is responding to your fans' comments and questions. You never know who might be reading your work, and comments are a great way to make an introduction. In some cases, it will be impossible to respond to everyone; however, do your best to respond to as many as possible. Your fans love your work, and you should show them appreciation in return.

Most importantly, when networking with other writers and your fans across all social media platforms, stay humble and do not feed the trolls. A screenshot is forever, so let your fans catch you at your best.

DIVE INTO WATTPAD'S NETWORKS

Take full advantage of the clubs, forum, writing contests, Hot Lists, and popular tags to find out what's currently trending on Wattpad. Here's a little about each.

The clubs are found under the "Community" tab on the Wattpad site, and they're organized by interest and genre. If you're new to Wattpad or you want to reach fresh readers or writers, these clubs are golden opportunities to make connections. You know exactly the people you'll run into because the clubs are focused. For example, there are clubs for horror fans and writers to talk shop about the publishing industry.

The forums are similar to the clubs and are located at www .wattpad.com/forums, but the difference is in the focus. The forums are wide open to discussion, and the topics aren't as organized. The advantage is that you can be specific about what you are looking for. It's not uncommon for writers to post a simple, "Looking for some friends, I'm new around here" thread. This type of straight-forward posting works best on the forums.

The writing contests are covered elsewhere in this book, but the networking benefits are valuable even if you don't win. Each contest focuses on a certain theme, so the entrants will all have something in common. Drop a note to entrants who caught your eye, and see what happens.

The Hot Lists rank the trending stories on Wattpad by genre. You can find them by selecting the "Discover" tab and choosing a genre. Head to the tab that says "Hot." There you'll find the top one thousand trending stories on Wattpad. In that same area, you'll see a list of the most popular tags that those trending stories are using. If you click on one of those tags, you'll see even more stories using that tag.

How do Hot Lists and tags benefit you? They give you a list of writers that you may want to watch or introduce yourself to for the sake of networking. You may want to use similar tags for your stories, too (tags are selected when you initially create a story and can be modified at any time). This will help you attract writers and readers.

STAY ENGAGED

At the bottom of each published chapter, add a short author's note. It could be as simple as "What did you think of this chapter?" or you could ask your readers what they think will happen in your next update. Engaging with your readers is awesome, and it's a great way to continuously grow your online audience.

Also, always remember to check back on your work and respond to the comments that are left by your readers. If you receive negative comments or are harassed by trolls, do not respond to them. Ignore them, and delete the comment. If you feel that it's necessary, you can mute them.

After you get into a routine of posting your chapters, continue to look for new writers to connect with on Wattpad. Comment frequently as you read other writers' stories, and vote for the chapters you enjoy. Join in the fun!

GROW YOUR COMMUNITY

Following these hacks is an easy way to network with other Wattpad writers and build your community both on and off of the platform. Wattpad writers are hands down the friendliest group of people in the world. Reach out, find your people, and have a great time growing your community!

About Kelly Anne Blount

USA Today best-selling author and Wattpad Star Kelly Anne Blount has more than seventy-five thousand followers on social media. Her Wattpad stories have been read more than twenty million times. She's contributed to Tap, Wattpad's new app for chat-style stories, where her work has been "tapped" more than fifty million times. She is a writer and reviewer for SpoilerTV, which has allowed her to develop an incredible network of film and TV stars.

Her Wattpad work, *Captured*, has been optioned and will be produced as a digital television series by Sony Pictures Television and Komixx Entertainment. She is also regularly invited to present seminars about social media at author events.

Stop by any of Kelly's social media platforms (@KellyAnneBlount) and her website (www.kellyanneblount.com) for announcements and information about upcoming releases and events.

CHAPTER 14

Writing Outside of English

By Ariana Godoy

On Wattpad: @cold_lady19

Connect with readers all over the world, no matter who you are or where you are from.

WRITE, WRITE, WRITE, NO MATTER YOUR NATIVE LANGUAGE

Speaking more than one language is an advantage in so many areas. That's also true when it comes to being a writer, especially on a site like Wattpad. Its sixty-five million users, as of this writing, come from diverse backgrounds, which is why Wattpad supports more than fifty languages. This spells excellent opportunities for writers from every corner of the planet to build their audiences.

I never considered writing in a language other than English even though I'm a native Spanish speaker. When I posted my first Spanish language story to Wattpad, it wasn't even in Spanish. I translated it to English. It did extremely well, with around thirty-five million reads. This motivated me to write my second story. That time around, I didn't translate it into English. When it also did well, I knew I had found something precious: my Spanish readership. My follower count on Wattpad now stands at 544,000, and I can say that more than half are Spanish-speaking readers.

OPPORTUNITY AWAITS

It is one thing to write in English and reach out to a single community of readers. But wouldn't it be amazing to reach out to multiple communities? I know for a fact that it is. Not only does it increase your opportunities to gain more followers, it also builds a multicultural following that will grow exponentially. You will have twice (or more) the opportunities to reach readers and twice the chances to attract publishers.

Of course, it can get confusing and time-consuming to write in two languages. To help you out, I'll give you the twelve most useful tips for using your bilingual advantage to its fullest potential while writing on Wattpad.

DON'T BE AFRAID TO TRY IT OUT

It may sound very simple, but some people are afraid to venture into Wattpad using another language, especially if it's not their native language. I remember reading the first comments on my new Spanish story with caution, fearful of criticism. I actually received lovely feedback.

Step out of your comfort zone, and try it. You already nailed the hard part, which is speaking more than one language. The writing will come easier. It takes a little getting used to, but remember that the more you write in a language, the more comfortable it will become. You'll be practicing the language while you're at it, so it's a win-win.

BE HONEST ABOUT YOUR TIME AVAILABILITY

Before starting this journey, you need to make sure you have time to give audiences of both languages the time and consideration they'd normally expect on Wattpad. That means keeping two sets of readers engaged, adjusting the story so that nothing gets lost in translation, writing or editing the same chapter more than once, and basically creating two versions of yourself as a writer. Once you go down the path of writing in more than one language, it can be overwhelming if you haven't considered your availability. Time management is extremely important when writing in multiple languages.

Picture a schedule in your head, write it down, and see if you would have enough time to keep up with the work you want to share with both audiences.

DON'T BE HARD ON YOURSELF

Be kind to yourself. I repeat: Please be kind to yourself during this process (not only in writing but in everything). You may not be the best at writing in two different languages right away, but I can assure you that you will get better every single day.

Mistakes are inevitable. They will happen, and you will learn from them. There's more about that in a later point. Positive thinking can motivate you and keep you going. Remember, writing is a constant process of growing and improving. Your attitude is crucial to pushing you forward.

KEEP IT SIMPLE

This goes along with time management. Don't jump into writing several stories at the same time in two different languages (I wouldn't even do that in one). You will only exhaust yourself and lose motivation.

Start with one story in one language, and go with the flow until you find a pace that suits you. Keeping up with the stories that you're writing is really important if you want to maintain your followers. I've seen how updating frequently has made a huge positive change in my statistics; reads and comments go way up. Therefore, don't start several stories at the same time if you cannot keep up with them. Doing so will only make the readers, and yourself, frustrated.

MAKE THE LANGUAGES OF YOUR STORIES CLEAR

Make sure to indicate the story's language right in the title if you have more than one version of the same story. For example, *The Boy (Spanish version)* and *The Boy (English version)* will help your readers easily find your stories in the language they want to read.

I'd also recommend keeping the same title on both (as I did with *The Boy*) and/or the same cover so people can connect the two. If you have bilingual readers, they can choose which one they'd rather read. On the other hand, you may have readers who want to practice their second language with your stories. If they've already read it in their mother tongue, they know what it's about and this may make it easier for them to read it in the second language. That gives your readers a learning opportunity.

BEYOND WRITING, COMMUNICATE IN BOTH LANGUAGES

Broadcast messages to your Wattpad followers in both languages. This extends to your social media. You want your followers to feel valued and to understand your messages without having to google them. They'll appreciate you more for taking the time to write the message in both languages. You'll show how you love and care for both communities, no matter the language. You'll also be giving a voice to your readers, telling them it's okay to come forward and talk to you in any of the languages because you understand and appreciate both of them.

FIND YOUR DOMINANT LANGUAGE

Most people who speak multiple languages have a dominant one. Identify it, and use it to improve your writing. Switch languages whenever you consider it necessary for a better result.

For example, if you are describing a fight scene and you feel your vocabulary in that particular scene is better in Spanish but you are writing this story in English, write the scene in Spanish and then translate it to English. Fix any translation errors, and your result will be an amazingly described scene. It's work, but it's worth it.

READ IN BOTH LANGUAGES

What better way to grow your vocabulary and spelling knowledge than reading? Reading has proven to enrich both. If you are used to reading in only one language, try the other.

I used to read mostly English books, but when I realized how limited my Spanish vocabulary was—even though it's my native language—I decided to read some Spanish books. I was shocked by how much my Spanish writing improved because of it. It solved some of my grammatical problems and streamlined my sentences. In addition, if you want to pursue traditional publishing at some point, it helps to see the story structure of a published book so you know what to aim for.

MAKE YOUR READERS PART OF THE PROCESS

One of the amazing things about Wattpad is the instant feedback you get. You can ask your readers to point out mistakes for you to fix. Sometimes when we write, the mistakes go unnoticed because we are too invested in the act of creating. Readers offer fresh eyes that can find things you didn't see.

Provide a safe, nice way to point out mistakes. For example, either in the comments or somewhere in a chapter, tell readers that if someone already pointed something out, there is no need for others to do so. Believe me, it can get repetitive very fast if you don't explain it that way.

WORK WITH YOUR MULTILINGUAL READERS

This goes hand in hand with my previous point, but I want to talk specifically about your bilingual readers. There is a very good chance that you have some bilingual readers, and they may come in handy when you are editing, proofreading, and revising in the language you feel less skilled in. If you're not sure about certain word usage, verb tenses, or phrasing, you can directly ask them.

I know it can be scary to let them know about your vulnerabilities in writing, but they won't see it like that; the Wattpad community is wonderful. They'll be eager to help and make your work even more awesome. That'll also give them a sense of ownership. They're helping to create your story, so they'll grow even more supportive.

BE YOURSELF

I know this is typical advice, but it plays an important role in building those relationships with your readers. You need to make those connections with them, to reach out. Share something about yourself in an author's note in every chapter (or every two or three chapters if that's your preference). I call it "leaving a trail of dots for them to connect with you and others." The simplest things can spark good conversations. As an example, I tell my readers about my favorite things or what I drink while reading their comments (usually coffee).

Wattpad has in-line comments—which is a feature I personally adore—so readers can comment on a specific line. I create dedicated lines at the end of the author's note with a question or a statement for them to comment on. It might be about the story or something random. It's an amazing way to interact. Reply to their comments, and get to know the people out there who are reading your work.

Remember to do this in all the stories, no matter the language. When I started doing these author's notes, I remember doing a lot in the Spanish stories. As a result, only my Hispanic readers and I grew closer. When I analyzed this, I realized that I needed to do this with my English stories to build those relationships, too.

CREATE NURTURING, KIND COMMUNITIES

Give equal love to communities of all languages you write in. Let them feel that you care equally for both and that they should expect the same commitment across the board.

Maintaining an update schedule helps a lot with this. I know sometimes we feel more inspired to write one story than others. I'm not advising you to mechanize your inspirational process, but you need to let readers know what's going on. A simple "Hey everyone, I'm just feeling more inclined to write this story/in [insert language here] lately" can go a long way toward maintaining your connection with readers. A short explanation will let them know that they are on your mind and that it was a matter of inspiration, not preference.

Also, reserve some of your time to watch the interaction that's happening between your stories and your board messages. See how your readers talk to each other, and model kind and respectful responses. They are following you because you created something they enjoy, and they want to participate in a nurturing, fun environment as much as you do.

You should also interact with other writers. Comment on their stories or on their boards. You may want to start with writers who are focused on the genre you write in since you already have that in common. Doing so can help promote your work and build unity.

EVERY LANGUAGE IS DIFFERENT

One of the most important things I learned while writing in both English and Spanish: Every language is different.

No, I'm not talking about the grammar, punctuation, and all that technical stuff. A language is much more than those components. Languages come with an incredible amount of nuance: the cultural background, the perspectives of that particular language-speaking community, the structure, and so much more. Metaphors, comparisons, sayings, and even humor vary in every language. There are words that, though superficially the same, carry completely different meanings. You have to be careful and constantly aware of this.

In my experience, something may sound hilarious in English in my head, but it isn't funny at all when I write it down in Spanish. Lots of metaphors and similes were lost in translation in my brain.

You need to set your mind to the language you're writing in to create something that is relatable and understandable for that readership. I usually ask myself, "Will this make sense if I only spoke Spanish?" or "Will this be funny?" If you're not sure of the answers, ask your readers for feedback. They will be more than happy to help.

NO REGRETS

Writing in two languages has been an amazing experience for me. It has been an absolute privilege to be able to reach two wonderful, supportive audiences. I've grown as writer and as a person. Immersing myself in two cultures and languages has been incredible. I love every single one of my readers, both English and Spanish speakers, from the bottom of my heart. Try taking a similar path if you speak more than one language.

Like I said, you already got through the hardest part, which is speaking more than one language. Applying those skills to writing may be a lot of work, but you will not regret it.

About Ariana Godoy

Ariana Godoy was born and raised in Venezuela and is a published author who now lives in the United States. Coffee, Korean dramas, and books are her constant companions. She writes on Wattpad in both English and Spanish under the username @cold_lady19.

CHAPTER 15

Fanfiction

WATTPAD'S WILD FRONTIER

By Noelle N.

On Wattpad: @hepburnettes

Take advantage of the built-in readerships that fanfiction offers.

On Wattpad, you will find some of the most robust fanfiction on the internet. From famous celebrities to fictional characters, blockbuster movies, award-winning literature, the latest Web series and comic books—you name it, Wattpad has it. If you're looking to expand your readership on Wattpad, diving into fanfiction is a great way to do it.

WHY FANFICTION AND WATTPAD ARE THE PERFECT MATCH

Fanfiction's popularity is due to the way Wattpad promotes the genre itself. Whereas fanfiction writers often struggle to find acknowledgment for their creativity and originality elsewhere, on Wattpad they are given space and consideration on par with original fiction writers. Discussion threads, fandom subcategories, and an official fanfiction profile (@Fanfic) are available platforms for writers to promote their books, learn more about fandoms, and increase their audience. Just like original fiction writers, fanfiction writers have a Hot List, take part in official writing contests (including the prestigious Watty Awards), and are eligible for opportunities from Wattpad to further their writing careers.

With a dedicated readership and writer base, fanfiction is one of Wattpad's biggest genres. That's saying something on a site with sixty-five million users, as of this writing.

NO, FANFICTION ISN'T "GUTTER" FICTION

For many years, some saw fanfiction as the gutter trash of the fiction world. They perceived fanfiction writers as piggybacking on someone else's characters and plots, as if these writers could not come up with an original story.

Thankfully, times have changed, due in large part to the way technology can connect fandoms. As an example, Anna Todd, Wattpad's biggest success story, started out writing fanfiction. After billions of reads, she scored major publishing and film deals.

GETTING STARTED

If you're new to Wattpad or fanfiction, it might seem daunting at first to jump into such a huge community. As a writer of both original fiction and fanfiction, I have firsthand knowledge of how difficult writing in the latter genre can be. But as with every new writing experience, all it takes is a leap of faith into one of the most exciting and vibrant communities on the site. Here are six things you'll need to know about writing fanfiction on Wattpad.

1. ENGAGE WITH FANDOMS

Is there a television show that you're currently obsessed with? Or are you a longtime fan of a book series? Perhaps you can't get enough of a band that's topping the music charts. Regardless of your preference, you would be hard-pressed to find a fandom that does not exist on Wattpad.

Fandoms are the key to fanfiction authors, especially new ones, gaining traction in the writing world. Here's why: Audience engagement is a staple for many Wattpad writers. At any one moment, Wattpad stories are being read, shared, discussed, promoted, and even posted about on social media sites. But in order to achieve that level of enthusiasm, a writer first has to gain readers' interest.

Fortunately, if you're a fanfiction writer, the interest in your work is already there. Within the fandom that you're writing in, there are readers eagerly awaiting a new book that they can add to their reading lists because they just can't get enough. All you have to do is engage with them.

One way to do that is on the Wattpad forums, where readers and writers come together to discuss their favorite movies, shows, music, books, and celebrities. Over on the official @Fanfic profile, contests take place that reward the winning writers with exposure for their stories. Creating a killer reading list dedicated to a certain fandom can help, too. And even in your work, a little interaction with your readers through the in-line comments can make a significant impact. Your readers will feel acknowledged, and they will be glad to spread the news about your fanfiction.

2. CATCH THE HYPE

There's a blockbuster movie that will be released next month. There's a highly anticipated album that's dropping this week. There's an ongoing television show that social media users can't stop raving about. What do you do?

Catch the hype.

Whenever there's new activity in the market for a particular franchise, the corresponding fandom's activity on Wattpad will also spike. In other words, within that fandom, there will be a surge in the number of readers and the amount of reading time spent on Wattpad. Seasoned readers will return for their fresh dose of fanfiction, while readers who've just signed up on Wattpad will likely be hunting for works catering to that fandom.

To prepare for this, it's important that you familiarize yourself with the subcategories and trends within fanfiction. For example, it is not enough to look at the DC or Marvel fandoms as a whole. You need to look specifically at *Wonder Woman* or *Spider-Man* because it's more likely that these subcategories will trend according to their respective theatrical releases in the market.

The other method that you could use is to anticipate a future release and publish your fanfiction according to that timeline. Say, for instance, your favorite K-pop group will be releasing an album at the end of the year. You have a solid plot in mind and a few prewritten chapters in stock. Instead of posting it during a lull, postpone it to coincide with the album's release because that's when interest in the band will peak.

The downside of catching the hype is that it can put you in the midst of fierce competition; many who write for that fandom will be publishing their fanfiction alongside yours. By the same token, succeeding under these circumstances will mean that the interest in your fanfiction is genuine. And if you're able to capture that pool of readers, you've got a good thing going for you.

3. CROSS RIGHT OVER

Crossovers are perhaps some of the most complex kinds of fanfiction. They require a blend of characters from two or more universes—such as *Star Trek* and *Star Wars* characters interacting with each other in a single fanfiction. You could even set *Star Trek* characters against the backdrop of the *Star Wars* galaxy, and that would constitute a crossover.

Writing a crossover requires you to have adequate knowledge of two or more fandoms. You need to do sufficient research to have a good grasp of two fictional universes and their respective characters. You need to imagine all kinds of scenarios and ask yourself many "what-if" questions. Would the rules of a certain world still apply if characters from the other stepped into it? If two protagonists from different worlds meet, would they complement each other or become adversaries? And if two villains meet, would they attempt to best each other, or would they work together to become even greater forces of evil?

It's therefore no surprise that for many fanfiction writers, crossovers are something that they're apprehensive about due to the sheer planning, world distorting, and character analysis they have to do. But for the bold and brave, crossovers can be your golden ticket to expanding your audience.

Consider the aforementioned point about engaging a fandom. That's your current pool of interested readers. Now multiply that number by two or three or however many fandoms your crossover entails.

That, right there, is your new audience.

Writing under a single fandom limits your number of interested readers. But when you write a crossover, you're growing your potential. Instead of tagging your work on Wattpad with only James T. Kirk or Leonard McCoy, you can expand your tags to include Han Solo and Luke Skywalker. That draws twice the number of readers interested in the former tags to your work.

But writing crossovers doesn't only have to be about expanding your readership. You may at times find yourself stagnant—writing the same trope over and over. You may have an equal love for two fandoms, but you're limited by time to write only one fanfiction. Or you may just want to explore a new aspect of fanfiction altogether.

So if you have a wild imagination and a fascination with challenges, crossovers might be the way to go. The hard work that you put into writing your crossover can prove to be very worthwhile in the end.

4. TAKE YOUR PICK

Surviving in one of the biggest genres on Wattpad isn't easy. After all, fanfiction authors do not write for their works to be published. They write to share their enthusiasm and make a name for themselves on the site.

It's not a bad thing to want an audience—every writer needs them. And many fanfiction writers choose one of two routes to expand their readership within the community:

- Establish a niche.
- Hop between fandoms.

The first entails making yourself known within the fandom for which you write. For instance, a writer could publish fanfiction after fanfiction solely for the *Supernatural* fandom. Regardless of the specific plots or characters that they write about, they're already building a reputation for themselves. Once you become a prolific writer for a single fandom, you should be able to maintain that steady flow of readers because your followers will direct new Wattpadders to you.

The second requires a bit of courage because you will be constantly going from subcategory to subcategory. Let's say that you're a huge fan of several television shows and, as previously mentioned, you're hoping to ride the latest wave of hype. You can write for the *Supernatural* fandom this time, but move on to *The Walking Dead* next, and so on.

It might seem a little scary at first when the majority of readers don't recognize your work since you've only contributed one book to their fandom. But each time you post within a different sub category of fanfiction, you're expanding your pool of readers— some of whom will follow you to your next work. And as you hop from one niche interest to the next in your stories, that pool will only continue to grow with time.

Both methods are equally viable. It's up to you to decide how you will make a name for yourself in the fanfiction community. Nevertheless, it's important to remember that consistent updates and new books are essential to generating reader interest, regardless of which option you choose.

5. KNOW THE BOUNDARIES

The parameters of fanfiction are generally wide, but there are several things to take into consideration.

One thing you should never do is disrespect the original author's copyright. If your fanfiction on Wattpad is based on an existing work or show, it's essential that you add a disclaimer in your foreword or synopsis that identifies the creator(s) of the source material.

The second is that you need to be aware of what is or isn't canon. Every fictional universe is created within a set of guidelines. If a fanfiction author traverses these boundaries, an explanation is required.

For example, it's canon that Harry Potter is a wizard. But if he's not a wizard in your fanfiction, then you're required to state that your work is an AU (alternate universe) in which, say, Harry Potter is simply an average guy in college.

While veering outside of canon allows fanfiction authors the freedom to create more original plots, doing so risks receiving more criticism. Plenty of fans have opinions about the way a certain character should be portrayed, especially since they often base their perception of the character on the original material. But what if you want to write a villainous version of Harry Potter—one who freely uses dark magic and eventually becomes a Death Eater? You need to brace yourself for readers who might not be too happy with that. And for the majority of your readers, who will be open to reading something fresh, you need to properly flesh out the reasons for his behavior in your fanfiction.

6. YES, IT'S WORTH IT

As someone who writes both original fiction and fanfiction, the common questions that readers ask me are: "Why not stick to original fiction? Why dabble with fanfiction when you know for a fact that these works can never be published?"

My answer is simple: practice.

Many writers write fanfiction simply because they're passionate about some corner of pop culture. But there are other writers who, perhaps, do not feel very confident about their writing. They need an avenue to improve their writing and experiment with new styles. And what better way to do that than with fanfiction?

Writing fanfiction allows you to take a step back and look at your writing as it is, without the pressures of submitting manuscripts or getting published. You are forced to pay attention to the setting of another writer's fictional universe and the nuances of their established characters. You must shape a plot that builds on the existing one, and you need to abide by the rules of that established world, all while creating your own narrative that distinguishes you from the original writer.

When you're done with your fanfiction and return to your original work, you'll be able to look at your writing from a fresh perspective.

You'll become more adept at world-building because you've already practiced by embellishing on someone else's. Your characters will no longer be one-dimensional—they will be multifaceted, with proper development and solid backstories. You will be bolder in your narrative because you have a style that's singularly yours and you have improved.

Additionally, walking the line between both can give you unexpected perks that other writers do not get. For instance, establishing yourself as both a fanfiction and romance writer will enable you to reach across two of the biggest genres on Wattpad. You will be able to incorporate romance elements into your fanfiction, as well as increase your proficiency in world-building, thanks to the practice you've had writing fanfiction. So if you're solely a fanfiction or an original fiction writer, all it takes is one step out of your comfort zone.

FANFICTION ABOUT FANFICTION

Suppose your fanfiction becomes popular enough that another writer asks, "Can I write a fanfiction based on your work?" Now, this would be fanfiction about fanfiction—one of the more complicated and rare forms within this genre.

Whether the person's request is accepted or not is the author's prerogative. Some fanfiction authors—like many published authors, in fact—are open to it, while others are not. But if the author answers in the affirmative, this presents a question. Who should the credit and disclaimer go to—the author who wrote the fanfiction in the first place or the author of the original, source content?

All credit and disclaimers should be attributed to the *original* author or creator.

It is essential to remember that fanfiction is an homage to the original work. Without the original creator's world, plot, and characters, fanfiction would not exist. Therefore, giving credit where credit is due is necessary.

START BUILDING

Writing fanfiction on Wattpad can be both challenging and rewarding, but it's worth a shot given its popularity on a site with sixty-five million users (and counting). Just remember that it takes time to research, draft, and plan out your fanfiction. It takes time to write a good work that showcases your best writing and the love that you have for the fandom. And it takes even more time to build a dedicated and loyal readership on Wattpad amidst the millions of users on the site.

It is essential, therefore, to embark on this journey with a positive mind-set. Think of fanfiction as a genre that is fun to write, something that you love to do, and/or as a means to improve your writing. And remember, no matter how many followers or reads you have on Wattpad, you can only go up from there. Welcome to fanfiction on Wattpad. Once you're in, you'll never want to leave.

About Noelle N.

Noelle N. is a pseudonym for an English major graduate who hails from Asia. On Wattpad, she writes both original fiction and fanfiction, has been privileged enough to win four Wattys, and maintains a pretty sweet status as an anonymous writer. Off Wattpad, she enjoys good music, great food, and spending time with her loved ones. More often than not, she writes because she wants to read something that she can't find elsewhere. As long as her work inspires someone, she's pretty happy.

PART 3

Building Your Writing Career

CHAPTER 16

Define Success, or It'll Define You

by Benjamin Sobieck

On Wattpad: @BenSobieck

Success is different for everyone. Reaching goals specific to your experience is what's important, not comparing yourself to other writers.

THE BAD NEWS

I have no idea what success looks like. Not on Wattpad or anywhere else in the writing world. None. I can't tell you what the concrete definition of success is because I'm not you, and I'm not sure I've achieved it myself. How's that for irony? I'm also the editor of this book.

The tragicomic truth at the heart of "success" and "making it" is that there is no truth. People will spend their entire lives trying to achieve success, and even the ones who do probably don't think they did. An individual's success is often only noticeable from outside of that person's experience, like a zit between the eyes.

That blindness is symptomatic of the writer's life, the penalty for practicing mental athletics in solitude. Writing isn't a job application with a definite "yes" or "no" at the end of the process.

It isn't licensed by the state (yet) and loaded with hoops to jump through. The words of "real" writers aren't separated from those of the "less real" writers, as if the opaqueness of ink at the printing press varies based on credentials. And even though there are trophies, there are no stadiums.

Because writing is a lifestyle, a frame of mind, an exercise in spirit, its metrics live outside the measurements of money and titles that normally apply to business and industry. Can you really assign a value to a story? No, because writing and reading aren't commodities like oil or gold. That's why a set definition of success is hard to come by. For that reason, I don't know what success looks like, and neither do you, Wattpad writer. Only the bitter, disingenuous, or mean-spirited would claim otherwise.

THE GOOD NEWS

The good news is that the nebulousness of "success" allows for writers to craft interpretations unique to themselves. Success is defined differently for everyone. To one writer, it may mean getting one hundred reads on a Wattpad story, and to another, success may mean receiving one million. For someone else, it may just mean completing a story. Often there isn't one goal but a series of goals. Some are small, and some are large, but they are all part of a process that can take a lifetime to play out. Taking this long view allows posting a 1,000-word short story on Wattpad to hold the same weight as nabbing a book deal with a major publisher. The old saying is true: Things are what you make of them.

What's important isn't that your achievements are on par with those Wattpad writers you admire. It's important that you set a reasonable goal and meet it, then hit a goal a few inches farther than that one, and so on. The only failure is staying put, so don't get discouraged when something doesn't work out. Keep writing, and celebrate your achievements along the way, no matter how small or large they may be.

Perhaps you've heard similar advice before, but it bears repeating. It's much more substantive and vital than some pithy words overlaid on a stock image of a mountain, and that's because it concerns the state of mind you need to be in before hitting the Wattpad trail hard. At times, the very nature of Wattpad's powerful technology makes it easy to fall into a pit of doubt and self-loathing. The number of reads, comments, and votes on a story are front and center. It's impossible to read a story or write one without noticing those metrics. Will one hundred reads on your story this Tuesday ruin Wednesday? Will your motivation dissolve along with your metrics?

BEWARE THE SPECTER OF METRICS

Remember, though, that success exists outside of metrics. It's tempting to use hard data to gauge how much traction you're gaining, but numbers can only represent so much of the picture. There are stories on Wattpad with millions of reads and nothing to show for it. There are also stories with a few thousand reads and a truckload of accolades, achievements, and advances to back them up. The reason why is a mix of numerous factors. Once you recognize that, there's no reason to let Wattpad metrics steer your internal dialogue.

Still, no one is immune to those jaded attitudes, including me. When I joined Wattpad in 2015, it was for two reasons. One was that I'd read about a presentation that a Wattpad staff member had given at a writing conference, and the site sounded interesting. Coincidentally, the mentions of metrics grabbed my attention. There's nothing like hard data to back up assumptions about where a piece of writing is headed. The second reason was that I'd hit a dead end with my fiction. It needed a home and a fresh shot. Wattpad made sense. I'll skip the parts about why my writing career hit a snag and how I was a little harder on myself than was necessary because the point remains the same. I had—and still have—

a definition of success tailored to my personal journey through writing. Hitting a roadblock didn't mean the end of the world. It meant that it was time to try something new. I'm now a Wattpad Star, I'm a Watty Award winner, and I can count many opportunities that have come my way after my reads took off.

I'm not pulling from a thought experiment or some glib self-help manual when I tell you these things. It happened to me. It wouldn't have, however, had I not kept my personal definition of success in clear view because the sound of other writers rocketing past my station in life was deafening. In 2015, many of my best writer buds were signing contracts with big publishers, visiting with movers and shakers in the entertainment industry, stuffing their bank accounts, and traveling the world. Meanwhile, I kept myself busy at home by giving away my work on Wattpad for free. Despite feeling happy for their achievements, it would've been self-sabotage to compare myself to those other writers. Had I let someone else's experiences set the benchmarks for my specific situation, my writing life would be completely different and you certainly wouldn't be reading these words.

WHAT CAN SUCCESS LOOK LIKE?

Keeping all of this in mind, there are patterns to how writers define a successful Wattpad experience. They typically revolve around five things, in no particular order:

- Attracting passionate readers who will follow them on or off Wattpad
- Securing opportunities with an agent, publisher, or partner
- Building robust communities of writers and readers around causes or topics (see chapter nineteen for more about this)
- Networking with other talented writers
- Having fun

Again, I'm not saying you need to choose one or all of those. It's worth noting how other writers approach Wattpad so that you can start to form the specifics.

As an example, I fall into the first and second bullet points. My goal is to build a platform of readers and leverage that into bigger opportunities. I'll keep the specifics to myself because you need to set your own goals.

On that note, write those specifics down, as in paper-and-pencil write it down. I don't know exactly how, but it helps. Would you believe that I did that very thing several months prior to winning a Watty and gaining entry into the Wattpad Stars program? It's true.

It's spooky how different your mind-set can be when you state an intention, write it down, and focus on the words on a regular basis. It sends a message to your brain to organize its contents around meeting that goal. I don't mean that in a supernatural, law of attraction way, although these concepts sometimes get framed that way. There is some definite, grounded psychology at play that occupies the same real estate as athletes' visualization techniques before an important event. It's no guarantee, but it optimizes your chances.

Shortly before I began work on this chapter, I posted an open question on my Wattpad profile page. I wanted to know what success looked like in the eyes of other Wattpad writers. I especially wanted to know the POV of writers who weren't Wattpad Stars like myself since they're paddling upstream more often than I am. Yes, there are advantages to being in the Stars program, and I'd be the first to admit that.

As expected, the responses varied. The one constant revolved around Wattpad being a tool or a path to something greater. I've selected a few responses to highlight here.

LL Montez (@LLMontez) saw value in the support of a community of writers, writing: "When I came in here, I knew no one.

Now I've made many friends—actual friends who are honest and supportive. That's the biggest Wattpad win."

Taking a wider view of where that support can take you, @Maeve Siverling wrote that, "Having your work adapted to something else, like a TV series or a movie would be considered a great success. The challenge then is to keep that engaged community of fans interested in those other adaptations."

Of course, success need not mean sitting in the banquet hall with glamorous Hollywood types. Melissa Luznicky Garrett (@MLGarrett) took a granular view by replying, "As long as I have one person who finds joy and entertainment in what I write … [someone] who can relate to my characters in some small or big way, I've done my job."

Not everyone felt as optimistic. @TheAlvarezChronicles cited the difficulty of both obtaining and leveraging reads on Wattpad, stating, "Real writers don't have to be successful on Wattpad for their writing life to mean something. Some of the best writers I have ever seen are on here, and no one reads them. Wattpad is a crapshoot. Never judge your writing by your success on it. You will get it wrong. Just write how your heart tells you to write."

I included that comment in this chapter because it's fair criticism. Does everyone writing on Wattpad go on to fame and fortune? Of course not, and I'm not here to convince you otherwise. It's true that some well-read Wattpad stories wouldn't fall into the category of Pulitzer Prize-winning literature. Some of them might even be my stories. It's also true that deserving writers and writing go unnoticed. The Wattpad experience isn't always fair.

However, none of that is endemic to Wattpad. Writers have levied these criticisms about the publishing industry since there has been a publishing industry. As far back as the first printed books, when a tiny scoop of elites monopolized literacy, nothing was fair. The democratization of writing ushered in by twenty-first-century technology is certainly progress, but it's still not immune from things like the Pareto principle, which dictates that about 80 percent of effects stem from 20 percent of causes. You can tweak those percentages up or down, but they don't matter as much as the general idea, because this lopsided phenomenon is present in almost every market on Earth. Therefore, you can't drop millions of writers into a Wattpad bucket and expect everyone to have the same experience. Some of it is talent. Some of it is luck. Some of it is a mystery.

You need to consider that with clear eyes because your path to success, wherever that might be, isn't going to feel fair. Heck, even when it's in your favor, it might not feel fair. That's why you've got to keep your focus wrapped tight around those individual goals and, again, define where you are on your own terms.

None of this is meant to discourage you, dear writer. You are actually at an advantage if you recognize the obstacles in front of you because you'll have a better appreciation of how to deal with them. When you expect walls, you can pack a ladder.

EXAMPLES

Let's get to the real rock stars of Wattpad, the writers who turned reads into reality. Remember, it's counterproductive to compare your successes to the following writers'. Still, it's helpful to see what is possible so you can dream big.

Anna Todd (@imaginator1D) tops the list as the original breakout star. As of this writing, 1.3 million Wattpad users follow her profile, and the reads on her stories are into the billions. The popularity of her After series on Wattpad morphed into a traditional publishing contract with Simon & Schuster. That propelled her into what looks a lot like the dream life of a full-time writer. If you've read about Wattpad writers in the news media, you've probably come across Todd's name.

Isabelle Ronin (@isabelleronin) worked up more than 170 million reads on her Wattpad story, *Chasing Red*. That landed her a major publishing contract with Sourcebooks, and two of her books hit shelves in 2017. Like many contracted writers who got their starts on Wattpad, her original stories remain available on the site to read for free. That may sound surprising, but it speaks to the way Wattpad works as an on-ramp toward building a readership that can be monetized elsewhere.

While Todd and Ronin nailed a traditional bull's-eye, some writers have seen their stories permeate other media. In 2018, Lauren Palphreyman (@LEPalphreyman) debuted a TV pilot through CW Seed for her story *Cupid's Match*. Twenty-four Wattpad writers, as of this writing, saw their works adapted into audiobooks via Hachette.

That should get you thinking about the possibilities. Your success doesn't have to flow from Wattpad to a traditional publisher and then to film adaptations or other initiatives as in years past. Intellectual property can be exploited in any number of ways right off the bat. At WattCon 2017, Wattpad's official event in Toronto, someone on Wattpad's staff told me that writers should think of themselves as creators more than writers. To wit, in 2017, Entertainment One, a distribution company based in Toronto, announced it would be partnering with Wattpad to source content for virtual reality projects.

These writers represent only a few of Wattpad's success stories. An exhaustive list would include millions of writers and every shade of achievement because once again, success has no hard-and-fast definition. It's soft and slow. What does success on Wattpad look like? It's up to you.

About Benjamin Sobieck

Benjamin Sobieck is a Wattpad Star and 2016 Watty Award winner. He's best known on Wattpad for *Glass Eye: Confessions of a Fake Psychic Detective*, the Watty Award–winning sequel *Black Eye*, and *When the Black-Eyed Children Knock & Other Stories*. Four of his titles have appeared on Wattpad Top 100 Hot Lists, all at the same time.

CHAPTER 17

Using Wattpad to Leverage Success in Traditional Publishing

By Sara Sargent

A presence on Wattpad offers several advantages when it comes time to make the leap into traditional publishing.

WHAT WATTPAD WRITERS HAVE THAT OTHERS DON'T

At any given time, there are thousands of websites, apps, devices, articles, and channels competing for young people's attention. It's a loud, crowded media world, which means it's more crucial than ever for publishers to cut through the noise with books that connect with readers. An author with a preexisting platform or fanbase is an automatic leg up.

WATTPAD CAN SEPARATE SIGNAL FROM NOISE

When young adult publishers consider whether to acquire a book by a new author, they often look at the author's social media following, particularly on Twitter and Instagram. A considerable following is helpful for two reasons: It shows that the author has opinions, expertise, or a compelling online voice that inspires people to follow and listen, *and* it shows that those same followers may very well be inclined to spend ten to twenty dollars on the author's future book. A considerable following demonstrates that you've already captured the cultural consciousness in some way and that you already possess the tools to cut through the dreaded noise.

What's important for publishers to understand about Wattpad is that it's more than a self-publishing platform; it's also a social network. Yes, writers from all over the world are self-publishing their work on Wattpad—but they're also connecting with readers and writers, building fanbases and brands. Popularity on Wattpad is like any other following on Twitter or Instagram: It demonstrates reach and influence. And beyond online reach and influence, it demonstrates the appeal of your manuscript. It's like a vetting process. When publishers see a lot of reads, positive comments, and a high ranking, it's a signal that there's something special about a book. The Wattpad community is a test group telling us what's working (and not working) in your book. There is no other mechanism like it.

HOW DO PUBLISHERS FIND WATTPAD WRITERS?

Publishers recognize that not all writers on Wattpad are looking for traditional book deals. For many writers, posting on Wattpad is about the joy of posting on Wattpad: the camaraderie of the community, the immediacy of the fan interaction, the mutable nature of the content.

For writers, on the other hand, who are looking to have their manuscripts picked up by traditional publishers, there are certainly best practices. First, in terms of how publishers find Wattpad books to publish, there are two mechanisms. The first and most common is that the wonderful folks at Wattpad go out on submission with a manuscript that's already posted online. Whether writers are aware of that process is handled on a case-by-case basis by Wattpad staff. Wattpad draws publishers' attention to a project, and it's considered an official submission (the same way that we receive submissions from literary agents). Another means of discoverability is that editors keep an eye on Wattpad themselves. They may pay close attention to the Wattys or simply poke around on the site, looking for books that are performing well. As I'll explain later, Wattpad has many advantages from a publisher's perspective, and that includes its ability to help an editor keep a finger on the pulse of popular YA fare.

HOW DO WATTPAD WRITERS FIND PUBLISHERS?

Another way for a publisher to find your piece is for you to submit it directly. When it comes to these submissions, it's important to do your research very carefully. A lot of publishing houses do not accept what we call "unsolicited submissions," or manuscripts that aren't submitted by a literary agent. It's important for you to determine which publishers accept submissions and which publishers do not. *Writer's Market* is one option for that research.

When submitting work to houses that welcome unsolicited submissions, it's key to use Twitter or a paid site like Publishers Marketplace to determine what kinds of projects certain editors are keen on based on the types of books they've previously acquired. Editors oftentimes specialize in (or have a strong preference for) particular genres. You wouldn't want to submit your paranormal manuscript to an editor who only handles realistic contemporary romance.

One trick is to look in the back of your favorite books and scan the Acknowledgments, where the author will usually mention their editor. And the most important thing to remember is that an editor's list of previously published books will tell you both what the editor likes in general *and* what the editor already has enough of. If your book sounds identical to another book the editor has published, that's a negative, not a positive. You want your book to fit into the wheelhouse of what an editor does on the whole, but you don't want it too similar to another project because editors can't have overlapping titles on their lists.

TAKING ANOTHER LOOK AT THAT WATTPAD STORY

Now, the manuscript evaluation process! The first note is that with the upside of data comes the downside of data. If you or your agent are querying a traditional publisher with a manuscript published on Wattpad and the ranking is middling, the comments are few, or the general engagement looks low, the publisher is going to take that into account.

It will be important to strategize on your own or with your literary agent. It might be good to include some positive feedback or comments from your readership to demonstrate that while your story may not yet have a giant fanbase, those who've read it have enjoyed it. The publisher will be interested in how long the story has been live on the site, whether you've published other stories (and in what genres) and how those have performed, and what edits you've made to your story since it went up. These suggestions aren't intended to be alarmist; it's simply good to be aware of how editors may assess prepublished works and use the information available to determine whether to take on a project.

HOW EDITORS LOOK AT WATTPAD STORIES

I think many—if not most—editors first read the query letter when they receive a submission, or they'll read the project first if they find it online. *Then* they may dip into the comments.

Editors want to evaluate manuscripts using their own assessment tools. We are guided by our instincts, and we rely on them first and foremost, rather than letting strangers' comments determine our decisions. This means that if there are indeed some negative comments on your story, do not worry that it will spell the end of your success with traditional publishers. Trust and believe in the process and in editors' abilities to judge for themselves.

PUBLISHERS WILL CHANGE YOUR WATTPAD STORY

Once your book is acquired, you will have to undergo what every contracted and soon-to-be-published writer must undergo: the editorial process. It's something that most self-published writers are unused to since they have been in charge of their own writing destinies up until this point (except, perhaps, when it comes to readers' comments).

A unique aspect of Wattpad, in terms of the editorial process, is that you and your editor have access to hundreds of comments throughout your manuscript that tell you what people think is working and not working. If the comments indicate that a certain section is lagging, then you and your editor can come up with a solution. And if the comments indicate that a certain section is really working, then you and your editor may consider amplifying it or incorporating elements of its success into other parts of the story. That sort of real-time feedback is not something editors get from brand-new manuscripts, and it can certainly help inform the editing process in all manner of ways. In addition, it will be beneficial to share with your publisher any changes you've made to the story, either on or off Wattpad.

HITTING BOOKSHELVES

When your main or originating publisher (called the "lead publisher") licenses the right to publish your book, they are doing so for a specific territory. If, for instance, HarperCollins is your lead publisher, Harper may license the rights to publish your book in North America, the British Commonwealth, or the entire world.

Under traditional circumstances (i.e., without the data provided by self-publishing), publishers must use their best judgment and intuition to decide whether a book is likely to find success in a given part of the world. With Wattpad, you, as the holder of the account, already have that information. Are you getting lots of comments from readers in the Philippines? In Iceland? In South Africa? Those metrics will show publishers that you are over-indexing in certain parts of the world, meaning that your story has global appeal and reach. It gives your publisher more incentive to pursue deals with publishers in those territories on your behalf, *and* it gives them hard data to use when pitching to those foreign publishers and convincing them to pick up your book. You are providing your publisher with invaluable data that will serve to make your book the greatest possible global success.

TURNING WATTPAD READERS INTO BOOK BUYERS

About six months before your book is published, your publisher will want to strategize with you about how to leverage your pre-existing base to maximize book sales. There will be considered discussions about how to handle the Wattpad content: whether to leave it up, whether to edit it, whether to put the complete and fully edited manuscript on Wattpad. Different publishers will have different approaches.

You also want the readers who already love you to buy your e-book for their devices or to go into bookstores and buy the physical copy. It will be useful for you to talk to your publisher about your fans (whom you know inside out) and discuss the best way to convert them from reading your book on Wattpad to spending money on it. Will your readers want you to be a purist, leaving the story mostly as is? Will they want a new ending as an incentive to buy this version? Will they want more content or an added dimension? You may not have these answers in place already; through various conversations with your editor, you will devise the optimal plan.

WHAT'S DRAWING READERS IN?

The copy you see on the flaps of a physical book or on retailer websites like Amazon is a joint effort between you and your editor. It has to be optimized to sound as compelling and appealing as possible to potential readers who have hundreds of books to choose from.

Have you noticed that changing elements of your summary or your copy on Wattpad meant more or less interest in your book? Does it seem like a certain aspect of your concept—the toe-curling romance, the thrilling twists and turns, the lyrical writing—is what's drawing people in? Your editor wants all of that information; it helps inform the best tack when it comes to enticing readers.

WHAT'S YOUR NAME?

One element that differs between Wattpad publishing and traditional publishing is the use of pseudonyms versus real names. On social media sites, members can assign themselves usernames that allow them to conceal their true identities. When it comes to traditionally published works, a small percentage of authors use pen names.

This is because, as I mentioned above, we want our writers to get out there and connect with the public and their readership. Sometimes this includes in-person appearances, and YA writers frequently make strong personal connections with the people who read their works. Unlike the level of remove on Wattpad, with our authors there's a lot more transparency between writer and reader—and typically that includes using your real name.

BRINGING IT BACK TO WATTPAD

Following publication, another possibility is posting additional content on Wattpad. Wattpad is a great place to post interstitial stories—prequels, sequels, supporting characters' POVs—that complement the core book. Publishers will be excited that you have a place where your fans already live and that Wattpad is such a natural home for related materials. It's a way to keep preexisting fans engaged and pick up new fans. Think of it as a marketing tool. As discussed at the very beginning of this chapter, anything you can do to increase your profile and the number of people interested in your work betters the book's chances of succeeding in the marketplace.

TRENDSETTING

There are also broader ways that the Wattpad platform can complement the traditional publishing process.

Typically, an editor receives manuscripts from agents, and the incoming flow for one editor might be anywhere from a few submissions to twenty submissions per week. Through the submission process, editors get a sense of what kinds of trends are percolating. It may take a handful of submissions over a period of weeks or months for it to become clear that a certain topic or genre (e.g., vampires, dystopian, fantasy, werewolves, contemporary romance) has surfaced in the zeitgeist. This is because, from where an editor sits, there are two types of trends: current marketplace trends (what's selling at this very moment) and author trends (what authors across the world are writing about and what will be selling in the future).

With Wattpad, we're able to see what's popular in the latter category in real time. We can see what stories are popular *right now*, which may help us predict the next wave or trend. It certainly tells us what thousands of people are spending their time reading! And that can open our eyes to new genres, inspirations, and ideas.

About Sara Sargent

Sara Sargent is an executive editor at HarperCollins Children's Books, where she publishes platform-driven fiction and nonfiction in the picture book, middle-grade, and young adult categories. Previously, she was an editor at Simon Pulse, an imprint of Simon & Schuster. Sara has worked with *New York Times* bestselling authors Laurie Hernandez, Abbi Glines, Ainsley Earhardt, Rosamund Hodge, and Lisa Maxwell; internationally best-selling author Lily Collins; National Book Award finalist Deb Caletti; and social media influencers Stacy Hinojosa (StacyPlays), Matthew Espinosa, and Arden Rose. She received her master of science in journalism degree from Northwestern University.

CHAPTER 18

Selling Books Available Outside of Wattpad

By A.V. Geiger

On Wattpad: @adam_and_jane

To drive book sales from Wattpad, forget sounding like a salesperson and load up on ... hummus?

Wattpad is a powerful tool for writers to turbocharge book sales. I started out as an amateur Wattpad storyteller in 2013 and climbed my way to a thriving career as a full-time author four years later. My young adult debut novel, *Follow Me Back* (Sourcebooks, June 2017), and the sequel, *Tell Me No Lies* (Sourcebooks, June 2018), both began as Wattpad stories before snagging a traditional book deal in North America, with translated editions selling in more than ten other territories. Meanwhile, my Wattpad new adult romance, *It's Only Temporary* (Hachette, August 2017), was released in audiobook format around the same time.

I consider my Wattpad presence the most important weapon in my book-marketing arsenal, but it's not some magic money-making machine. Over the course of my debut year, I learned a ton about what works—and what doesn't—when attempting to translate Wattpad reads and votes into book sales. In this chapter, I'll share my four key rules.

RULE #1: GET OUT OF THE MARKETING MIND-SET

First and foremost, writers must approach Wattpad as a place to share stories and engage with a community of readers. Sales are a side benefit, not the primary goal. As a writer, you must always bear in mind that your readers joined Wattpad for two reasons: to access stories for free and to share their own stories with others. A large segment of Wattpadders have no interest in paying for content, and they may face barriers that prevent them from buying books. Many are teenagers who don't have credit cards. Others are from parts of the world with limited access to bookstores, libraries, and retail websites.

For writers selling published work, these readers still have tremendous value. They hold the power to make your work stand out in a sea of books. Every set of eyeballs can increase a story's popularity and its likelihood of being discovered by other readers, some of whom *will* have purchasing power. For this reason, every Wattpad reader should be viewed not as a potential sales lead but as a potential member of your marketing team, helping to extend your story's reach.

With that philosophy in mind, let's get down to business. There's one particular marketing tactic I see on Wattpad all the time, and it's always a recipe for failure. In fact, I see this mistake so often that I consider it my second key rule.

RULE #2: DON'T POST AN EXCERPT; GIVE READERS A FULL MEAL

This rule may come as a surprise to seasoned authors. Teasing with an excerpt is Book Marketing 101, right? Give away the first chapter for free, hook the reader, and then use a call-to-action to close the sale. This book-marketing tactic works like a charm on retail websites, where potential customers can "Look Inside" virtual pages of a printed book or download sample chapters from an e-book. So why doesn't it work on Wattpad?

To answer that question, let's take a step back from the book business and consider an analogy. Think of your book excerpt on a retail website like a salesperson giving away free samples of hummus at the neighborhood grocery store. It works in the store. Not everyone who takes a sample will turn into a paying customer, but no one will find it strange to see you standing there hawking your wares.

Now imagine you're at a friend's house, attempting to sell your hummus to the guests at a potluck dinner party. There you stand with your little plastic sample cups, flanked on all sides by an array of homemade casserole dishes. (Are you cringing at the awkwardness yet? You should be.) Many other people at the party have brought their own dish to share. If you offer them a tiny helping of hummus and ask them to pay for a full dollop, they won't whip out their wallets. More likely than not, they'll give you a dirty look and move on to the full-sized dishes being offered all around you.

As counterintuitive as it may seem, if you want to sell hummus at a potluck party, you have to plunk down a whole vat of the stuff and let the guests help themselves to an unlimited portion. Let them rave to their friends about how delicious your hummus tastes, until a whole gaggle of partygoers have gathered by your dish. Then stand around, and make small talk. Try the other dishes. Exchange cooking tips. Once you've established a rapport, tell the story of how your homemade hummus was recently discovered by some gourmet food packager—and now it's available for sale at the local grocery store.

"Amazing! I'm so happy for you," your new friends will say. They won't buy any hummus at the party. They probably didn't even bring their wallets. But a few of those partygoers might find themselves in the market for hummus sometime soon. When they see the refrigerator case packed with twenty different brands, yours will be the one they put in their cart.

The same concept applies when selling books on Wattpad. Don't offer a tiny sample. Share a complete book, and give it away without so much as a whisper of money changing hands. Once that story has found a large audience, then offer a related published product available for purchase. Package it professionally, and make it available in stores where your Wattpad readers shop. Then, the next time your readers are in the market for a book, yours may be the one they recognize and buy.

RULE #3: SERVE READERS A HEARTY HELPING, BUT WHET THEIR APPETITES FOR MORE

"But wait!" I hear the naysayers shouting. "There's a big difference between hummus and books! You can eat your fill of hummus and still be hungry the next day. But a story, once read, has already been experienced. Why would anyone shell out money for a book they read for free?"

This is a valid concern. Whether you're self-publishing or working with a traditional publisher, there is a second ingredient your "hummus" must contain. The book you make available for purchase needs to have some added value beyond the version you posted online. There are various ways to accomplish that task, and I've experimented with a few of them. I'll share three techniques and how they each applied to my own portfolio of work.

Option 1

Make your completed Wattpad story available for purchase in a different format.

Works best for:

- Popular stories in high-traffic genres
- Authors with limited time

Sometimes a Wattpad story breaks through and achieves mass popularity. If you browse the list of books in huge genres like romance or teen fiction, you'll see plenty of read counts in the tens of millions. I found myself in the enviable position of writing one such book with my new adult (NA) romance, *It's Only Temporary*.

In Fall 2015, the story trended up on the romance Hot List, bringing in a whirlwind of new readers. *It's Only Temporary* soon leapfrogged all my other works to become my most-read Wattpad book. As thousands of reader comments accumulated, I noticed a trend: A growing legion of devoted fans came back to reread the complete story over and over again.

The opportunity to publish was staring me in the face, but I had a problem. I had a freshly minted book deal on a totally different book, and I couldn't commit the time to work on both projects at once. My answer came along when Hachette announced a new line of Wattpad sourced audiobooks. With a deal from Hachette, I spent a few days on a single round of copyediting before the publisher produced the book in audio format only. The final product was the exact same story that my Wattpad readers knew and loved but with a professional narrator bringing my words and characters to life.

The audiobook format created a new product with added value for my fans who had already reread the Wattpad version multiple times. The same idea could be accomplished in print form simply by hiring a professional cover designer and putting out a self-published collector's edition, available on a print-on-demand basis. Such a product might only appeal to a small fraction of the story's Wattpad audience—but with a large audience, a tiny fraction can add up to a steady stream of sales.

Option 2

Flesh out your completed Wattpad story with substantial additional content in a for-purchase version.

Works best for:

- Moderately popular stories in any genre
- Authors with months or years to invest in the publishing process

What about a story that isn't mega popular? If you find yourself with a read count in the thousands, don't despair. You can still use Wattpad to launch a published version, but you'll need to roll up your sleeves and do some work.

My teen thriller, *Follow Me Back*, originally gained popularity in the Wattpad mystery/thriller genre. It trended to the No. 1 spot on the Hot List in early 2015, but success in mystery/thriller translated to a much smaller read count than a popular story in romance. With under a million reads, I knew I needed to do more than simply repackage it in a different format.

As soon as I completed the Wattpad version, I embarked on a time-intensive offline editing process. I took my 65,000-word Wattpad draft, added 25,000 words of new scenes and then cut the whole thing down to a tightly paced 70,000-word final package. The project took multiple rounds and months of work, but the end result had ten chapters of added material that never appeared on Wattpad. When Sourcebooks released the book in 2017, I had no problem creating demand for the published version. My original Wattpad draft still provided a complete and satisfying story for online readers, but the added chapters gave fans a tantalizing reason to buy the paperback or e-book. Combined with an attractive new cover and an affordable price point, I had all the ingredients in place for a successful book release.

Option 3

Post a complete spin-off novel, novella, or short story that features the same characters and world as your for-purchase novel.

Works best for:

- Any book available for sale outside of Wattpad.
- Authors unwilling or unable to post the for-purchase novel online.

My experience above can work for any writer, self- or traditionally published, who is willing to put in the time and effort. Problems can sometimes arise, however, when traditional publishers are involved. Some publishers require authors to take down their Wattpad version before a book hits the market, for fear that the free story will cannibalize sales. If you find yourself in that position (and the publisher doesn't respond to your long-winded story about hummus salesmanship), there is one other strategy you can try.

In my case, I found myself with some free time in October 2016, nine months before *Follow Me Back* was slated for release. With Halloween around the corner, I had an idea for a scary spin-off story that would be set in the same world but focused on a minor character. I spent two weeks churning out a 10,000-word short story titled *Whatever You Do, Don't Read This*. I posted it in the horror genre, and I included an author's note explaining how it related to my forthcoming novel.

This spin-off story gave Wattpad horror readers a bite-sized free sample of my writing without the perils of posting an excerpt. Did the story result in any sales of my published book? I have no idea! It certainly didn't *hurt* my sales, and it may have introduced my work to some new fans.

Whichever option you choose, you will eventually have a product available for sale, and you'll have to ask your Wattpad readers to buy it. Tread carefully. Always remember that the readers on the other side of the screen view you not as a salesperson but as a peer.

RULE #4: STICK TO MARKETING TACTICS YOU WOULD USE IN PERSON WITH REAL-LIFE FRIENDS

Let's return to the potluck dinner party. You've laid out your hummus, and it's a hit with the crowd. The partygoers have wiped the platter clean, and they're clamoring for more. Now you need to let them know about the store-bought version coming to a supermarket near them.

If you jump straight into a sales pitch, your audience will drift away in search of better small talk. Instead, tell the crowd a story. Share how your product came to be—how a self-taught home chef made it in the competitive hummus-making business. Was it hard? Were there obstacles to overcome? How did you feel when you realized your lifelong dream of professional hummus-making had come true?

In Wattpad terms, don't just announce that your book is coming out. Tell your readers the story of how it happened. Let them feel like a part of your publishing journey, and thank them for the reads, votes, and comments that helped bring your publishing goals to fruition.

Once your readers know about your book, the next step is to build excitement. Don't drop an announcement the day the book goes on sale. Make your readers wait, and give them a reason to buzz with anticipation. A preorder campaign can work well in the two months prior to publication as long as you keep it lighthearted and entertaining. For *Follow Me Back*, I created a raffle with a prize package of inexpensive items that "belonged" to my fictional main characters. The grand prize cost me less than twenty dollars, but it felt both meaningful and humorous to Wattpad readers who knew my characters almost as well as I did.

Chatty storytelling posts and preorder campaigns are both good ways to communicate with readers in the weeks leading up to the release date. While your audience is waiting and brimming with excitement, you can harness their enthusiasm to spread the word about your book far and wide. Marketing ideas that work well for this purpose include giveaway contests to win advance copies of the book and fanfiction/fan-art contests. In both cases, readers must share content about your book on their own Wattpad accounts or other social media in order to be eligible for a prize.

HAVE FUN

Whatever else you do, the most important component of your marketing plan should always be fun. Stay engaged with your readers. Write more stories. Hold chat sessions. Respond to messages and comments. Get to know your readers on a personal level, and let them truly know you in return. Your Wattpad readers come from an incredibly vibrant and enthusiastic community. If you embrace them, they'll love nothing more than seeing one of their own succeed.

About A.V. Geiger

A.V. Geiger is followed by hundreds of thousands of readers on Wattpad, where she writes contemporary fiction under the username @adam_and_jane. Her debut novel, *Follow Me Back*, was an international sensation in summer 2017. The sequel, *Tell Me No Lies*, was released in June 2018. She lives in New Jersey with her husband and twin boys.

CHAPTER 19

Wattpad as a Tool for Advocacy

By Tahlie Purvis

On Wattpad: @TahliePurvis

The same Wattpad features that can make a story popular can also spread a message or idea.

MORE THAN JUST STORIES

Because Wattpad can quickly reach scores of readers across the globe, stories can stretch far beyond the boundaries of a narrative, taking on a completely different tone and purpose. This might be something as simple as a particular message that you want to share with a large group of people, a call to action, or an idea whose time has come. Regardless, the same tools that allow Wattpad stories to gain traction can also be used for these purposes.

START A CAMPAIGN

Not long ago, the ranks of writers on Wattpad put out a call for more diversity in books. Seeing this surge in advocacy motivated me to come up with a campaign that would promote physical diversity within books.

At first, I was unsure what I was going to do with the idea. I considered other social media platforms until I realized that I didn't necessarily need to pursue this idea independent of Wattpad. Wattpad may be grounded in literature that caters to young readers, but the site is also a social media platform. Millions of people come together on the site to share ideas and thoughts, and they interact with each other daily. My campaign is linked to literature, so I decided that Wattpad was a suitable base for my campaign.

A BIT ABOUT #FREEYOURBODY

At the time I created it, the goal of my campaign, #FreeYourBody, was to inspire authors to write books with characters that were different from the single generic body type (physically attractive, able-bodied, Caucasian) we see continuously in books and other media. All someone has to do is walk outside and notice that everyone looks different. There are different body sizes, skin colors, and conditions, from vitiligo all the way down to something as simple as acne. Literature doesn't always show this diverse physicality found in the real world. #FreeYourBody was an initiative to give writers the confidence to write about these complex and needed characters, and to create a pool where readers could easily find books linked to the campaign and connect.

STARTING THE CAMPAIGN

I proceeded to create a profile on Wattpad for the campaign. I came up with the name and then reached out to followers of my books to share with them what the campaign meant. As a social site, Wattpad is focused on interaction, so I mentioned that I wanted people to write their own books that depicted physically diverse characters. On Wattpad, books have tags that are similar to hashtags, and books with a particular tag attached to them appear in related searches.

I asked people to tag the books they submitted for the campaign with #FreeYourBody. This kept the campaign cohesive but still open and accessible on a site as large as Wattpad. I also created a small sticker that featured a circular image of the campaign logo for people to put on their books. As covers are often the key element that initially attracts a person to a book, I believed this would be the best way to raise awareness of my movement.

I wasn't sure what to expect since there had only been a few initiatives like this in the past. However, my doubts and worries were soon allayed. Within a couple of weeks, the #FreeYourBody profile had motivated thousands of followers and hundreds of authors to use the tag. It was overwhelming and honestly quite surprising to see. I hadn't imagined that my campaign would resonate with and connect so many people.

It became clear that people are on Wattpad to read stories that they connect with and are inspired by. As long as they form an emotional attachment to a certain type of book, they will follow it. For my campaign, it wasn't a story that connected or inspired them but a message: It's time to diversify characters' physical traits.

BEYOND WATTPAD

The moment I knew the campaign had become successful was when an employee of Wattpad contacted me and asked if I would be open to talking to media outlets about the campaign. She mentioned that my timing for the campaign aligned perfectly with the media's diversity coverage. From there, #FreeYourBody was covered by multiple media outlets, such as *Huffington Post Canada*, *Seventeen*, and *The Washington Post*, with Wattpad HQ supporting me along the way.

STARTING YOUR OWN CAMPAIGN

The one thing that I have learned through #FreeYourBody is that campaigns can't be executed passively, especially in the early stages. You can't create a campaign and then sit back and expect it to do all the work. There is a great deal of marketing to be done because word of the campaign must pick up steam somehow.

You also have to keep the audience interested. One way I did this was by rebooting the campaign, which included revamping the logo. I also created a contest to promote the books using the tag. I put together a collaborative book featuring Wattpad Stars and the #FreeYourBody community that was filled with pieces promoting body positivity.

Galvanizing people to continuously interact with a campaign is the easiest way to success. It's hard for others to overlook it.

DO CAMPAIGNS NEED TO USE STORIES?

A blank screen is a blank screen, and that's what's staring back at you when you start to create something new on Wattpad. That means that new work on Wattpad doesn't need to be driven by narrative. Each chapter does not necessarily have to be what's traditionally thought of as a chapter. They can be updates about the campaign, instructions, or blog-style posts.

In the same way, Wattpad user profiles can be used in a variety of ways. I turned one into the #FreeYourBody campaign page, and others have created magazines and contests. I didn't create characters, chapters, or novels for my page, even though these are things usually associated with Wattpad. Instead, there was a profile, a logo, and a hashtag, and my page fit in perfectly.

Remember that at its core, Wattpad is a site for sharing. Yes, people mostly share stories, but ultimately what you share is up to you.

WHAT IF YOU START A CAMPAIGN AND NO ONE NOTICES?

An advocacy campaign could be made with the greatest intentions in mind, yet it's possible that no one will hear of it. When this happens, it is likely due to the way that the organizers present the campaign.

If the name of the campaign is not memorable or is irrelevant to the campaign's goal, then it's going to struggle to pick up steam. A hashtag might also become diluted if it matches or is similar to an existing hashtag, so check other social media platforms before committing to one. When you do find one, stick to it across Wattpad and all other social media accounts. Using a single hashtag in this way is the best method for leveraging social media.

Next is the goal. The way you word and present your idea for the campaign must be concise, short, and compelling. A few sentences should explain the entire campaign in one go and result in an immediate understanding of the movement's purpose. The goal for #FreeYourBody is in the "About" section of its Wattpad profile: "#FreeYourBody is a campaign by @TahliePurvis (est. Oct. 19, 2015) to help promote the acceptance of body and skin types, conditions, disorders, and illnesses that are not usually depicted in books."

If you have a clearly stated goal for your campaign, it shows that you have confidence in your vision and are sincere about what you're trying to do.

Lastly, appearance is key. The campaign has to look inviting. As with books, people judge first impressions.

Wattpad profiles have a place for a profile picture and a background image. I felt that it was important to associate #FreeYourBody with a specific color. I made the logo for the campaign baby blue. This same color was used in the profile picture of the logo, in the background image, on the stickers that people can place on their book covers, and on all of the campaign books' covers. This made the campaign memorable and compelling.

KNOWING WHEN TO QUIT

As of this writing, I've operated #FreeYourBody for just over two years. During that time, I ceded management of the campaign to a Wattpad Ambassador (@Ambassadors). Ambassadors are volunteers who work with Wattpad to make it a safer and better place. I still oversee activities and initiatives, and I have the final say on everything that happens, but giving up the day-to-day duties was a necessary step because singlehandedly running a campaign that had amassed more than eleven thousand followers became a difficult task.

Besides, advocacy campaigns never really end. I think that each becomes a continuous effort. If my goal were ever fulfilled, then the campaign should remain a place to share and celebrate works of diversity. That said, it's important that you don't delete your campaign's account. Even if it ends up being inactive, the campaign should remain visible because the idea should remain accessible.

HERE COME THE HATERS

An understandable concern standing between a Wattpadder and starting a campaign are the trolls. Luckily, trolls are rare, and I attribute that to the fact that Wattpad works hard to create an inclusive and safe environment.

As far as dealing with trolls, a campaign account is different from a personal account. I would not respond on #FreeYourBody in the same way that I would on my writing account. When you are responding as the campaign, you must think of it as a business where you are the owner. Look at what the person is saying, and seek out any useful or constructive comments. If the comment proves to be constructive, then reply kindly. Do not be overly personal, but do not be cold. If the comment holds no use for you or the campaign, then it is easiest to delete the comment or "mute" the offending commenter.

A SUPPORTIVE CULTURE

Trolls aside, you'll find that Wattpad has nurtured a supportive, enthusiastic online community right from the start. Because of this, the best way to approach Wattpad is to view it as something more vital than just a place to read or write. Wattpad itself certainly does.

See Wattpad as a host, and see your ideas as projects that the site can help elevate. If you view Wattpad as a means to connect with people, then your ability to use it in ways beyond stories is almost limitless.

YOU HAVE SOMETHING TO SAY, SO SAY IT

Wattpad is a site for creative people with something to say. All you have to do is open up your mind, log on to Wattpad, and begin.

About Tahlie Purvis

Tahlie Purvis is a student living in Canada. She won a 2015 Watty Award for her short story, "The Girl He Left Behind," and became a Wattpad Star. She has written branded content for companies such as TELUS and Netflix.

CHAPTER 20

The Wattpad Stars Program

by Tim Johnson

On Wattpad: @Tim

The Wattpad Stars program taps the best and brightest writers for exclusive opportunities. It can happen to you, too.

WHAT IS A WATTPAD STAR?

A Wattpad Star is a writer who has proven that they have the potential for something bigger. Whether that means being published, seeing their ideas brought to the big screen, or just being extremely influential within the Wattpad community, they have something special and Wattpad wants a direct relationship with them.

LETTING THE STARS SHINE

The term "star" is really a perfect name for this program. With four hundred million glittery stories sparkling away in the Wattpad universe, it can feel like you have an astronomical chance of receiving recognition and being given the opportunity to truly shine.

However, that is not the case! Wattpad brings in new Wattpad Stars regularly, giving these writers professional writing opportunities, speaking engagements, and ongoing writer education. In this chapter, I will explain how to become a Wattpad Star and the benefits of being one.

Not long after my story *Cataindar: The Discovery* reached the number one spot in Wattpad's action genre, I was granted the opportunity to become a Wattpad Star. A few years later, I joined Wattpad as an employee, so I've seen the benefits of the Stars program as a Wattpad user and as a staff member.

It's been an incredible journey that has taken me all around the world. I've met Wattpadders who work full-time jobs as Hollywood writers, and I've watched friends go from Wattpad authors to *New York Times* bestsellers. Working at Wattpad has given me the chance to see how we use data, interact with the publishing industry, and stay at the forefront of digital storytelling. My time as both a Wattpad Star and a Wattpad employee has been incredibly fulfilling, so I am excited to share with you some information I have gleaned from the experience.

HOW TO BECOME A WATTPAD STAR

There is no cookie-cutter way of becoming a Wattpad star. Writers are chosen by the Wattpad team for many reasons, and there is no official application process. However, there are some key things that Wattpad is *always* on the look out for.

1. RISING POPULARITY

Seeing a steady rise in your popularity and reads on Wattpad will always be important, since trending stories are flagged by Wattpad HQ as ones to investigate.

2. POSITIVE ENGAGEMENT

Are you a force for good on the platform? Wattpad HQ is looking for amazing and inspiring people to work with. If you have a positive influence and interact with your readers and the Wattpad community in a kind and genuine fashion, that goes a long way.

3. AN AMAZING STORY

Wattpad HQ is searching for stories that are special. That means unique stories with great characters and exciting plots. Wattpad HQ also searches for stories that touch on current trends or interests that are prevalent in the media, as these are stories that could have a huge audience.

A great story that is well written and high ranking *will* capture Wattpad's attention. As a staff member, I now know how powerful Wattpad data is in helping furnish us with interesting stories on the platform sometimes months in advance of stories achieving a high ranking.

A great example is *Chasing Red* by Isabelle Ronin (@isabelle ronin). Wattpad knew that story would be a hit almost a full year before it reached the number one spot on the romance Hot List. It accumulated more reads and comments than any other story on Wattpad in 2016. Today, the story has been read more than 180 million times. Ronin's story has been published in several languages around the world.

Another example of a data-detected success is from Wattpad writer Kara Barbieri's (@Pandean) *White Stag*. She posted *White Stag* (think *The Hunger Games* meets *The Lord of the Rings*) on Wattpad in 2016. Wattpadders spent 6.5 times more hours reading *White Stag* than any other fantasy story on the platform! That led to a three-book deal with St. Martin's Press.

These are *exactly* the kinds of insights that the publishing and entertainment industries are looking for. This helps them decide to explore these Wattpad stories so they can make them into the next *Riverdale*, the next *Game of Thrones*, or the next *Stranger Things*.

WHAT ARE THE BENEFITS OF BECOMING A WATTPAD STAR?

Wattpad Stars have been granted access to a host of opportunities. Here are five big ones.

1. PUBLISHING OPPORTUNITIES

The opportunity that many are excited about is the chance to be traditionally published. Wattpad works with major publishers around the world who are looking for fresh stories with built-in audiences. One example of recent publishing success is *Textrovert*, which was written by Lindsey Summers (@DoNotMicrowave) on Wattpad under the title *The Cell Phone Swap*. This story is about two teens who accidentally swap cell phones and begin flirting. The Wattpad community loved these spirited characters, and the story garnered 100 million reads. This launched Lindsey Summers into the Stars program and led the story to be published by KCP Loft (Kids Can Press).

2. TV/MOVIE ADAPTATIONS

Not long ago, Universal Cable Productions (UCP) sought out original ideas for its next TV show. It wanted page-turning stories with a heroic lead character that would keep viewers on the edge of their seats. Wattpad partnered with UCP, and Stars had the chance to submit their ideas for this new TV show. The winning entry, unannounced as of this writing, could be optioned by UCP for adaptation to the small screen.

Keep in mind that adapted stories are not always traditionally published first. Because of Wattpad's network of partnerships, there are many opportunities for writers' works to be transformed into digital media, virtual reality, audio, and games.

3. BRANDED CAMPAIGNS

Wattpad provides Stars contracted writing opportunities through the Wattpad Brand Partnerships team. This team helps brands and new movies market to Wattpad's audience. These partnerships give our Stars the chance to write great stories for a brand or an upcoming movie. For example, Wattpad stars were commissioned to create stories set in the worlds of *Midnight Sun* (2018) and *The 5th Wave* (2016) as a way to build anticipation for those releases. There's more about branded campaigns in chapter twenty-three of this book.

4. ENGAGEMENTS

Wattpad is often presented with speaking opportunities at entertainment conferences, writing festivals, and literary events around the world. That's not to mention Wattpad's own live event, WattCon, which takes place in different cities around the world. Wattpad offers up these opportunities to our Stars to help them network in the publishing and entertainment industries, increase their social presence, grow their audiences, gain confidence in their speaking abilities, and educate the world about Wattpad.

5. ONGOING EDUCATION

The Wattpad Stars program also acts as an incubator for professional development. Stars receive access to a dedicated website called the Stars Portal, a Wattpad Stars e-newsletter, the Stars Slack channel, and Google Hangout sessions hosted by Wattpad HQ and guest speakers. This helps Stars stay up to date with trends in the publishing and entertainment industries.

Additionally, the Wattpad Stars team utilizes personal branding specialists who coach select Stars on building their brands. One exciting aspect of this is the opportunity to work with professional editors who ready their work for traditional publishers, television shows, movie adaptations, and more.

STARS IN THE MAKING

As you can see, the Wattpad Stars program is full of valuable opportunities. It continues to expand regularly, so Wattpad writers should feel encouraged to keep writing, engaging with their readers, and updating their stories. Who knows? The next Star could be you.

About Tim Johnson

Tim Johnson works for Wattpad as part of the Brand Solutions team. He's also the Watty Award–winning author of *Cataindar: The Discovery*.

CHAPTER 21

From Wattpad to Hollywood

by Tim Johnson

On Wattpad: @Tim

Wattpad Studios connects writers with content creators beyond the site, including publishers and television/movie producers.

Wattpad Studios is an exciting part of Wattpad's vision to entertain and connect the world through stories. If you're a writer, Wattpad Studios could be the thing that launches you into the big time. If you're a reader, Wattpad Studios is one of the best ways to see your favorite story come to life.

THE FUTURE OF STORYTELLING

Wattpad Studios started with a belief: The future of entertainment will be driven by communities of storytellers and backed by powerful data and insights. Aron Levitz, head of Wattpad Studios, summed it up as follows: "Wattpad deals exclusively in the one thing that powers the billion-dollar entertainment industry—original and compelling stories. As the largest and fastest-growing platform for stories, we can easily spot the voices that resonate with audiences around the world and the *stories* that have an established fanbase."

At Wattpad, he often mentions that we don't know what will be the dominant way of consuming stories in the future. It could be through augmented reality, virtual reality, enhanced audio services like Alexa, location-based apps like Pokémon GO, or holodecks. But what doesn't change is this—the world needs incredible stories. This is important to note because Wattpad is naturally disruptive. Although right now we cater to the current paradigm, we are anticipating the ways that storytelling will change.

HOW DOES WATTPAD STUDIOS WORK?

At the heart of it, Wattpad Studios connects entertainment and publishing executives with the stories you love to read and/or have written. This means Wattpad uses a combination of data and community insights to turn your stories into traditionally published books, movies, and TV. In turn, the entertainment industry can find stories with the greatest chance of commercial success through an existing fanbase.

Wattpad Studios is divided into specialized areas, and they all work in concert with one another. They are:

- **THE WATTPAD STARS PROGRAM**
  - Whenever you hear someone at Wattpad talk about our writers or Stars, they will often reverently utter, "Without them, none of us would be here today." This is how important the writers are to everyone at Wattpad.
  - Wattpad Stars are the most promising writers on the platform. These storytellers are the engine of Wattpad. They understand how to craft stories that drive mass engagement. Wattpad Stars give brands, publishers, and Studios access to a massive built-in audience. See the chapter about the Wattpad Stars program for more information.

- **WATTPAD BOOKS**

  - Wattpad Books connects traditional book publishers with millions of readers around the world to promote works to a new audience, test out story ideas and concepts, and gather reader feedback in real time. It's a pretty awesome way of leveraging our massive reading and writing community.
  - Wattpad plans to continue to collaborate with the largest publishing houses in the world to turn top Wattpad writers' works into global megahits. In 2017, three *New York Times* bestsellers started on Wattpad. We expect this trend to continue!

- **WATTPAD PRESENTS**

  - Wattpad Presents is a partnership with networks and producers to turn stories into content for television. Wattpad worked with the TV channel TV5 in the Philippines to create the series *Wattpad Presents*. This show takes a Wattpad story and airs it over four episodes sequentially throughout the week. It became the second-biggest show in the Philippines after *Amazing Race Philippines*.

- **WATTPAD INSIGHTS**

  - Earlier in this book, I spoke about the importance of data, but I can't stress enough how ahead of the curve this allows us to be when we are studying trends in popular culture.
  - Our data teams are constantly tracking what's resonating on the platform in order to predict larger trends for the entertainment world. We can home in on massive entertainment movements like cannibal mermaids, or roller-skating werewolves or mpreg through tracking uploads, shares, comments, and much more.
  - We leverage this through partnering with entertainment and publishing executives. They can subscribe to trend re-

ports that identify and analyze the types of content (genres, themes, subjects, etc.) that are making waves on Wattpad. They can also access IP reports that identify the top trending IP on Wattpad, as well as those hidden gems that we know are just waiting to become the next breakout hit.

PARTNERSHIPS IN ACTION

Wattpad Studios partners with outside companies in a variety of ways, and that equals more opportunities for Wattpad writers. Here are some examples from television, digital entertainment, and traditional publishing.

Television Partnerships

eOne, an entertainment distribution company, is one of Wattpad's most recent partners, currently on the lookout to turn a Wattpad story into a megahit. What constitutes a megahit? To put it in context, eOne Television's current lineup of original and acquired content includes *The Walking Dead*. Here's what Jocelyn Hamilton, the president of eOne, said about the partnership: "The powerful data and insights from Wattpad will allow us to tap into the new generation of authors and give us early access to captivating proven stories and characters." Wattpad Studios also partners with Universal Cable Productions (UCP). UCP developed fan favorites like *Battlestar Galactica*, *Mr. Robot*, and *Suits*. It's actively seeking programming based on Wattpad content, too. That's how Wattpad is working with the TV industry, but remember how we talked about new ways of consuming content?

Digital Partnerships

A great example of a digital video opportunity is *Cupid's Match* by Lauren Palphreyman (@LEPalphreyman). Wattpad worked with Tongal, a community of filmmakers, and The CW, a broadcasting company, on this project. Tongal created a series of trailers based on the story, and the Wattpad community voted for their favorite. That will be turned into a digital pilot, which could be turned into a full CW series. Building on this momentum, Wattpad also pitched *Cupid's Match* to traditional publishers, and the story will now be published in several different countries.

Partnerships with Movie Studios

Wattpad teamed up with The Coup Company for a pitch contest that gave Canadian filmmakers a chance to pitch ideas based on Hollywood writer Josh Saltzman's collection of creepy short stories, *Strange Yarns*. Winning entries were then turned into short films capturing these creepy tales forever.

Partnerships with Publishers

Wattpad hasn't slackened on the traditional publishing front either. It partnered with Hachette on an epic deal to bring Wattpad stories to life as audiobooks. In 2017, Hachette Audio produced twenty audiobooks based on Wattpad stories written by people from all over the world and will continue to publish more in 2018. For more detail, here's Ashleigh Gardner, head of partnerships for Wattpad Studios: "We love seeing the worlds and characters Wattpad storytellers create come to life in different ways. The Hachette Audiobooks: Powered by Wattpad partnership gives the Stars of the Wattpad community a unique chance to have their stories narrated by skilled actors and distributed to people beyond the Wattpad platform. Wattpad stories have been successfully produced as books, television shows, and movies. Now people will not only be able to read and watch Wattpad stories but also listen to them. Storytelling has never sounded so good." Hachette was just as pleased. "We are equally excited to be working with Wattpad to amplify the audience and broaden the channels of discovery for their unique brand of storytelling via audiobook editions," said Anthony Goff, senior vice president of content development and audio publisher at Hachette Book Group. Getting the picture yet?

HOW TO GET INVOLVED WITH WATTPAD STUDIOS

Share your best story on Wattpad. Take risks, and be bold with your storytelling. Don't ever think you're too young, too old, not smart enough, or too into the details; you just need to write your story and set those characters free. Throw yourself into your work, and write for yourself; you will find your audience.

Enter contests. Instead of competing with four hundred million stories, you're competing with just a few thousand. Contests are always worth a shot and offer great practice for your writing.

The truth of it is this: Wattpad is always looking at content. If your story is catching fire on Wattpad, someone at HQ is checking it out. If and when Wattpad contacts you, be polite, responsive, and professional.

WHAT DOES WATTPAD STUDIOS LOOK FOR?

Wattpad Studios is looking for strong voices, storytellers bold enough to entice the masses with the promise of plot twists, unreliable narrators, awesome revenge, and steamy romance. Essentially, Wattpad Studios is looking at everything, but let's also be realistic. Trends are a thing. It's hard to see vampire stories coming back right now, so entertainment companies aren't currently seeking them out.

That said, there are, as the president of eOne mentioned, three things that Wattpad Studios places front and center when working with partners. They're the same things that Wattpad Studios focuses on when looking at Wattpad writers for these deals.

1. DATA INSIGHTS

These translate into the ability to know what plot twists your audience loved or what can be cut, for example. With all our data, partners already know the fan-favorite characters and also perhaps the ones that might not make it into the final production. They can see what's trending. This ability to see the trend is gold to entertainment companies—and can mean incredible opportunities for Wattpad writers.

2. A NEW GENERATION OF AUTHORS

Fresh voices. Hollywood has served up a lot of the same for a long time. The industry knows it needs to uncover fresh new voices whose experiences may have been historically marginalized. That includes authors of color, authors of diverse ethnicities, authors from the LGBTQ+ community, and authors with different abilities. These are the voices that make up the Wattpad community and that the world needs to hear more of.

3. CAPTIVATING, PROVEN STORIES AND CHARACTERS

And this is what it all comes down to. Note "captivating" *and* "proven." Wattpad can help take a little of the guesswork out of the "But is this really going to find an audience?" question that these companies often have. They are seeking stories that are going to grab people, episode after episode. They are looking for big, established, thoughtful worlds that will bring people back, season after season. They want worlds that are so well built that they suck you in and won't let you go. The same goes for characters. What is *The Walking Dead* without Rick? Or *Game of Thrones* without Jon Snow?

WATTPAD STUDIOS IS WORKING FOR WRITERS

What it all boils down to is that there's a team of dedicated, passionate people at Wattpad who can make the kind of connections in the entertainment and publishing industries that you dream about. All you need to do is keep writing on Wattpad and building an audience. And if you see a message in your in-box from someone from Wattpad Studios, know that you're in for some great news.

About Tim Johnson

Tim Johnson works for Wattpad as part of the Brand Solutions team. He's also the Watty Award–winning author of *Cataindar: The Discovery*.

CHAPTER 22

Win or Lose, Contests Offer Big Opportunities

by Amber K Bryant

On Wattpad: @amberkbryant

Hone your craft, build your platform, and win career-building prizes with Wattpad contests, but also keep in mind that you don't have to win in order to gain something.

Writing contests can be intimidating. They entail putting your work out there and knowing you are doing something for which you, by definition, will be judged. Still, there are tantalizing lures dangled in front of writers' eyes in conjunction with entering a contest: prizes, honor, accolades, and exposure.

The Wattpad contest experience offers a host of benefits that go far beyond these accolades and can offer even the most intimidated writer a cherished seat at the Wattpad community table. Some are informal, while Wattpad officially sanctions others. They might range from "Write a short story based on this movie" to "Caption this comic book panel." All such contests may potentially empower a person to be noticed by the sizable Wattpad community, making them well worth your time as a writer.

I have participated in contests on Wattpad as an entrant, a judge, and a host. Having won several high-profile contests (including the Wattys, R.L. Stine's Fill in the Fear Contest, and three contests hosted and/or judged by Margaret Atwood) and having lost just as many, I can attest to the fact that the benefits of participating in contests go beyond what you receive if you win. Contests are a wonderful way to immerse yourself in the community, get to know your fellow Wattpadders, build your platform, and practice your writing craft.

In this chapter, I will speak to the advantages of participating in contests and explain the different sorts of competitions offered, including Wattpad sponsored/brand-partnership contests, community-profile contests, and user-hosted contests. Lastly, I will talk about the contest experience itself.

IT'S NOT ALL ABOUT WINNING: THE BENEFITS OF PARTICIPATION

Writing can be a solitary experience in which we spend hours in our own heads attempting to extract ideas and place them on the page in a cohesive, engaging manner. If you're seeking out a story-sharing platform like Wattpad to help showcase your work, it means you want more than to write in a bubble devoid of others' input. The Wattpad community can help nurture your love of writing as well as foster a better understanding of the writing craft. When you enter a contest on Wattpad, you are doing so with a group of fellow contestants. Congratulations, participant! You are no longer alone.

When newer Wattpadders ask how they can gain readership, one piece of advice I keep at the ready is to participate in contests. Reading other entrants' stories and leaving encouraging, positive comments will often result in a reciprocal show of support from those participants. Lasting friendships may be forged from the simple act of reaching out and acknowledging their efforts.

One of the people I met through Margaret Atwood's Freeze-Dried Fiction Contest has become very dear to me. Even though that event took place several years ago, we still communicate regularly. It doesn't matter to me that neither of us won that contest. Her friendship and the friendship of several other participants were the biggest rewards I could receive. Through mutual encouragement, she and I have gone on to participate in and win subsequent Atwood contests. Each contest experience was enriched by our friendship.

Another benefit is found in the writing process itself. Perhaps the contest is in a genre you're not as familiar with and forces you to stretch your thinking a bit. Maybe its prompt has made you put together a concept you would otherwise never have dreamt up. Whatever the case, when you produce a piece tailored to the requirements of a competition, each story you write is an opportunity to improve and grow. Whether the contest calls for a 500-word flash fiction horror story or a 30,000-word romantic-adventure novella, you will emerge from the experience a better, more capable writer for having challenged yourself.

In addition to Wattpad users and fellow contestants, judges will be reading your story. For some of Wattpad's most high-profile contests, famous authors, television showrunners, and editors of major publishing houses will have their eyes on your work. Scary? Maybe it is, but it's also a thrilling prospect and certainly an incentive to deliver your best material.

Before the contest results are revealed, you've already won more than you may realize: You've written a story, been brave enough to click the "Publish" button, interacted with other contest participants and readers, possibly even had your work read by industry experts, and presented yourself as someone willing to be an active member in the Wattpad community.

KNOW YOUR CONTEST

There are three primary types of contests hosted on Wattpad:

- User hosted
- Community profile hosted
- Official Wattpad sponsored

Anyone can host a contest. During my first year on Wattpad, I ran a microfiction competition through my profile. This allowed me to interact closely with contestants and gave those people an opportunity for exposure when I promoted them to my fanbase. While you may find the occasional user-hosted contest with large prizes, often these are small-scale operations. The main prize is the honor of having your story (or fan art or cover design, depending on the contest) selected. Even if a shout-out and honor are your only prizes, user contests offer you a plethora of the benefits listed in the previous section.

Do be aware that users will occasionally present contests for which there is no real endgame, that are merely meant to draw attention to the hosts. Also, steer clear of contests that offer prizes in violation of Wattpad's Code of Conduct, such as vote trading.

Community-profile-hosted contests are usually run by Wattpad Ambassadors working for Wattpad's official community pages, such as @ScienceFiction, @Romance, or @ParanormalCommunity. These contests rely on volunteer ambassadors to come up with the contest parameters, create a contest guidebook, monitor questions, gather prizes, and judge entries. Community profiles are increasingly collaborative and now offer contests that span multiple profiles, meaning more exposure for the contest winners.

Wattpad-sponsored contests are those officially hosted by Wattpad and/or its brand partners. The Wattys, the largest online writing contest in the world, falls into this category, as do contests Wattpad offers in conjunction with production companies and networks, corporations, publishers, or individual authors. These are large contests widely promoted by Wattpad, and prizes can be substantial. Winners have seen their stories turned into digital shorts, have received publishing contracts and television deals, and have been awarded cash prizes and other swag.

THE OFFICIAL WATTPAD CONTEST EXPERIENCE

The Logistics

Wattpad offers many contests in partnership with an amazing array of well-known companies such as Hulu, Netflix, and the Syfy channel. This next part will focus on what it's like to participate in such a competition.

Each contest has a set of rules that are laid out in a contest guidebook posted on the brand partner's verified profile page. Read the rules closely, following prompts, word-count restrictions, and other requirements. This is paramount. If you have questions about the contest guidebook, ask an ambassador for assistance.

Wattpad offers a growing number of contests, and many will be open to users of various locations and ages even if a given contest is more restrictive regarding who may enter. It can be disappointing to discover that you don't qualify for an intriguing contest because you live outside of the geographic locations dictated in the contest regulations or are younger than the age requirement. These restrictions are usually beyond Wattpad's control. While Wattpad wants as many people to participate as possible, their brand partners might cite legal issues or requests that necessitate restricting who can become a contestant. Regardless, you can opt to write for the competition anyway and still receive all of the benefits that come with participating (outside of winning). Keep your eyes peeled because the next amazing opportunity may be announced any day!

Write by the Rules

If you've made the decision to participate, the next step is to write your story. Do not go over the designated word count, and make sure that you are following all guidelines. Write the best story you can. While every person has her own writing habits and quirks, personally, I never look at the other entrants' stories until mine is completed and posted. I don't want to be influenced by what someone else has done. The creative process is one particularly anxiety-inducing stage of the competition, when self-doubt wants to pop up and say, "Hello." While I don't read others' entries at this point, I do often call upon a friend, preferably one familiar with the genre or topic, to beta-read my entry. A fresh pair of eyes can do wonders when it comes to catching typos and inconsistencies.

Contest Etiquette

As soon as I've posted my story, I dive into the other entries. I've mentioned this before, but it's worth repeating: Read as many of the other entries as time allows and leave thoughtful, positive comments on them. Camaraderie between participants is essential to making your contest experience a positive one. The feeling that you are all in this together and that you are rooting for one another's success is the essence of what community is all about. Relish this. This is not the time to be critical of another's work unless that criticism is specifically requested. Always find something reassuring to say, even about a story you may not have liked, or say nothing at all if the only other choice is to be negative. If you catch a typo, private-message (PM) the author and mention it within a polite note. A few kind words can make someone's day.

People are nervous enough about how their stories will do without having unconstructive, petty, or nitpicky criticism dappled throughout their comment threads by fellow contestants. Remember, you are in competition with these people: Being rude, ungrateful, or negative will earn you a reputation as an insecure writer who denigrates others to preserve your own ego. This advice carries over into all of your Wattpad interactions, but it is particularly true in the contest environment, where good sportsmanship is expected without exception.

Proper contest etiquette extends to the winner's circle and beyond. Being able to congratulate winning writers when you are on the losing end shows that you're a supportive and gracious community member. If you do win, expressing gratitude to other writers in the contest, as well as to the judges and contest hosts, likewise casts you in a positive light. If you've made friends during a competition, decide whether you want those relationships to extend beyond the announcement of the winners and then act accordingly.

Networking

You will no doubt discover some gems among the other entries. Resist the urge to compare your own work to theirs. That's the judge's job, not yours. Instead, while you await the contest results, get to know the writers who created these gems. Gush over their stories if the gushing is warranted and authentic, and then see what other stories they have on their profile. If something intrigues you, give it a try and be sure to let them know that you're enjoying it. Again, be authentic. Comments don't have to be paragraphs long, but they should emphasize the fact that you are reading and grasping the storyline.

Reach out! Message your fellow competitors with your thoughts on the contest. Connect with them as someone who is also waiting and hoping. The wait may seem to take forever, but it is easier if you are doing so with friends.

The Multistep Contest

Most contests involve submitting a story and then waiting for results, but some have multiple phases. These may include a voting round or a quarterfinal/semifinal process. Multistep contests are designed to whittle down the number of entrants to a select few. Be aware of all that a contest entails before you enter so that you are prepared to participate from beginning to end. If there are voting rounds, that usually means your story must get a certain number of votes from Wattpad users within a certain time frame in order to proceed to the next round. This can be particularly challenging if you are new to Wattpad and don't yet have a large platform, but a solid story that is supported by your Wattpad followers and especially by fellow contest participants can still succeed. Remember that you may ask people to vote on your story, but you cannot bribe them or agree to vote on their works in exchange for a vote on your own.

A contest with finalist rounds is one where the judges will narrow down the list of winners to a select, small group of candidates. Making it to a semifinal list is a huge achievement. Use the opportunity to promote your story. It may not win the grand prize, but it has still been acknowledged by judges for its worthiness.

Winning and Losing Contests

There is an undeniable thrill when you are told that you've won a contest. Your work has been recognized, and that's something to be enormously proud of. Prizes are fun, and the prizes of larger contests may be downright extraordinary. Beyond the prize you win, you have a line on your writer's résumé that may help lead to more contest wins, features, and even agent or publisher interest.

If you've won one of Wattpad's official contests, you'll be informed via private message or through the e-mail you have linked to your Wattpad account. Depending on the contest, there may be paperwork or a contract that needs to be filled out. Wattpad will walk you through this process and will answer any questions you may have.

Contest norms dictate that there are few winners. Disappointment over losing is understandable, but this must never prevent you from trying again. My own strategy for dealing with contest dejection is to allow myself one day to mourn what could have been. The next day, I pick myself up, put the disappointment behind me, and get back to work. If you have another project waiting in the wings to which you can turn your attention, the sting will quickly be replaced by motivation.

Wallowing for too long is counterproductive. It's not realistic to assume that you'll win each contest you participate in. No one achieves a 100 percent victory rate in the writing world. Rejection is part of a writer's life, and contest judging is a subjective art. You will fare better if you don't take a loss personally and acknowledge that every storyteller, no matter how gifted, is told "no" far more times than he is told "yes." Don't forget that participating in contests is its own victory: The rewards that come from making friends, sharing in the community-building process, and knowing you have the courage to try something that may not have the desired outcome belong to everyone willing to take the plunge.

GO FOR IT!

There are friendships, a sense of connectedness, improved writing skills, exposure, increased readership, and the possibility of prizes and glory awaiting you if you decide to enter the world of Wattpad writing contests. Contests are part of the fabric that weaves stories and the people who tell them together on Wattpad. The only thing you need to do to be part of that is have the courage to try.

About Amber K Bryant

Amber K Bryant is a Wattpad Star, a multi-genre author, and a librarian living deep within sasquatch territory in Washington State. She has co-authored a short story with R.L. Stine, won a Watty for her novella, *Unseen*, and won three contests judged by Margaret Atwood. When not glued to her keyboard, Amber can be found spending time with her husband and son, hiking, gardening, and searching in vain for the elusive sasquatch.

CHAPTER 23

Writing for Wattpad Campaigns

By Darly Jamison

On Wattpad: @Monrosey

If you're not charging anyone to read your stories, can you still make money from your writing on Wattpad? Yes, you can.

IT'S A NEW ERA

It's no secret that digital advertising in the form of native ads (content that includes a brand's message) has become the foundation for most marketing campaigns. Every time we open our laptops or use an app on our phones, we are bombarded with products and brands both familiar and new to us. But do we always engage with those endorsements? Several untraditional yet successful ways for strategists to use Wattpad to reach their target audiences can greatly benefit both the writer and the brand. In this chapter, I will go over four of them: brand campaigns, contests, outside opportunities, and advocacy campaigns.

BRAND CAMPAIGNS

Like any social media platform, Wattpad is not just a place to communicate and form relationships with people from all over the world—it is also an effective tool for business promotion. Marketing and advertising become a whole lot easier when companies know what consumers are looking for, and by utilizing Wattpad's top influencers, who are already familiar with reader trends, they can reach a wider audience quickly and effectively, with satisfying results. With Wattpad brand campaigns, marketers are able to monitor what is being viewed on the site, how often, and for how long, which allows them to see what is working and what isn't.

When Wattpad partners with a brand campaign, it goes big. Disney, 20th Century Fox, USA Network, TNT, Coca-Cola, Netflix, General Electric, and Frito-Lay are just a few of the companies behind brand campaigns that ran on Wattpad. These campaigns give opportunities to authors to earn money for their work. At the same time, brands can access targeted advertising, which is achieved through entertainment rather than a typical ad.

Wattpad brand campaigns have a unique ability to reach sixty-five million active users each month, as of this writing. Both writers and readers consist of, but are not limited to, Millennials and Generation Z, who are quick to interact with content created by their favorite Wattpad authors. And using those authors to help maximize awareness of various products differs from traditional marketing strategies by connecting readers with their go-to brands in ways that are relevant and interesting to them. It's important to keep in mind that consumers do not want to be *sold* a product. What better way to reach them than by giving them what they are already looking for—authentic and meaningful entertainment?

Authors and their loyal fanbases also participate in spreading the word by simply commenting on and sharing work that touches or inspires them, which is something they are already doing on the site. The eagerness of readers pushes these stories up the ranks on the Hot Lists, which in turn will make them more visible on the site and better able to create connections.

I have been a member of the Wattpad community since 2014 and have been very fortunate to work on many different brand campaigns. In early 2017, I was contacted by Wattpad and given the opportunity to create a 500-word story supporting female empowerment, inspired by Margaret Atwood's best-selling classic novel, *The Handmaid's Tale*, which premiered as a serialized television show on Hulu in April 2017. Other authors were also invited to write commissioned pieces for the promotion, and the stories were then added to a sponsored reading list that appears on the Hulu profile page. The release of those stories kicked off a writing competition that was open to all Wattpadders, asking them to produce the same kind of pieces. And the prize? Ten entries were chosen from the extensive list of submissions to be included in an anthology curated by Margaret Atwood herself!

In addition to the campaign I worked on with Hulu, I have also been commissioned by Warner Brothers on two separate occasions to create custom content to promote their premieres. For the first project, I was asked to write a 2,000-word story about a high school urban legend for the release of a horror flick titled *The Gallows*. In the second, I wrote a 10,000-word story inspired by *Unforgettable*, a drama that revolves around an unstable divorced woman who terrorizes her ex-husband's fiancée. With the *Unforgettable* campaign, I received valuable feedback from Warner Brothers that helped ensure the story I wrote met the company's needs. In 2018, Paramount pictures comissioned me to write a 500-word story inspired by the movie, *A Quiet Place*.

Customized material and contests are only a couple of ways for partners to advertise; they also have the ability to browse through the millions of existing stories and choose their favorites to appear on sponsored reading lists, which are featured on brand profiles, including ones that best fit their themes. In all cases, Wattpad itself coordinated the brand campaign. There isn't a place on the site where writers go to apply for these opportunities. Wattpad contacts writers individually. Some writers may be selected over others for various reasons, but know that the more professional and ubiquitous you are on Wattpad, the more likely you are to be chosen. Matching a writer's genre and style to the brand campaign's goals is also important. Work hard, keep your readers engaged, and be the kind of writer a major brand would feel comfortable working with on a campaign. Those brands need to know they're in good hands.

Not only do these opportunities help brands reach larger audiences, but writers benefit from the experience as well. Aside from the monetary aspect, writers are extremely enthusiastic to be a part of the campaign process and work hard to create relevant material they hope Wattpad, their partners, and readers will enjoy for many years to come. They are then able to devise worthwhile stories that contribute to their personal portfolios and add the experience of working with such high-profile companies to their résumés, which they use when submitting to literary agents and publishers.

ANOTHER TYPE OF BRANDED CAMPAIGN: CONTESTS

Branded content is not the only way to reach consumers. Some brands and publishers sponsor writing contests inspired by movies, television shows, books, and more. Readers and writers, no matter their stage of writing development, are challenged to write short stories inspired by these brands. As with the aforementioned Atwood contest, prizes may also be offered.

For example, a partnership between Wattpad and Lionsgate, the studio responsible for the movie *Wonder* (which premiered in theaters in November 2017), invited Wattpadders to create short works of fiction for the #ChooseKind campaign. The top-three lucky finalists then had their stories developed into film shorts to promote kindness. How amazing is that? A digital short was also made from the winning story in the #BattleTheBeast contest sponsored by Syfy to promote *The Magicians*, and the winner received $10,000!

In addition to prizes like those, publishing contracts have also been awarded to hardworking Wattpad writers. Harlequin hosted the So You Think You Can Write contest on the site, searching for new voices in romantic fiction. Simon & Schuster chose ten lucky fairy tale–inspired short stories to appear in an anthology called *Once Upon Now*. And my own debut novel, *Strawberry Wine*, was the result of winning The Write Affair contest promoted through Kensington Publishing. For more information on contests, see the previous chapter.

OUTSIDE OPPORTUNITIES

Sometimes companies outside of Wattpad offer branded campaign opportunities directly to writers. As writers post their work and their reads, votes, and comments continue to grow, brands may stop and take notice. It's not unheard of to have brands approach a writer with a business proposal. It is important for authors to take precautions. They must do their homework before signing on with these companies. This should involve asking to speak with previous and current contracted writers. If an author is sent a contract, she (or her lawyer) should be sure to read over everything carefully, ask plenty of questions, and have a clear understanding before she signs any contracts.

One way to learn if a company is legitimate is to do an online search. If results show negative or suspicious activity, that would be something to make note of. Reputable brands should have an official website to browse through that showcases their affiliations and partnerships, and if contacted, these partners should recommend working with said company.

If writers are still unsure, they should contact an ambassador (through @Ambassadors) or submit a request through the Help Center.

Writers on Wattpad who have managed to gain hundreds of thousands, if not millions, of reads on their stories have been known on occasion to query an outside brand themselves, just as one would query an agent or publisher. They may negotiate a deal to collaborate on a brand campaign that they and the brand work together to develop. Due diligence is necessary here, too, and writers may want to seek professional legal counsel before signing anything.

ADVOCACY CAMPAIGNS

Wattpad campaigns do not only come in the form of brands and products. A large representation of advocacy movements run campaigns as well.

There are several ways for Wattpadders to show support and give a voice to issues closest to them. The community is rich in active and passionate projects, such as the ambassador-run profile @NoMoreBullying, and user-run accounts that focus on several different topics, including diversity, healthy relationships, human rights, positive body image, mental-illness awareness, and everything in between. These campaigns sometimes have brands attached to them and may take the form of contests.

Many campaigns have a hashtag associated with them (for example, #LaterHaters and #RiseAbove) and stickers that can be applied to story covers. They encourage Wattpadders to create content that fits a specific criterion as part of a contest.

Because Wattpad is such an active place, writers and readers often create campaigns of their own that don't involve brands. The benefits include making both professional and personal connections to grow your own network, which can lead to fulfillment of your long-term goals.

PUT IN THE WORK

In all honesty, I have to say that writers get out of their Wattpad experience what they put into it. Being an active member on the site has opened so many doors for me, and the connections and accomplishments, both professional and personal, are more than I could have ever hoped for.

Starting out on Wattpad can be more than a little intimidating, considering there are millions of writers and even more published stories out there, but the drive to become better at our craft and the determination to add to résumés and portfolios can sometimes lead to opportunities we never dreamed possible. Working with major companies on campaigns that help advertise different products and resonate with consumers on an intimate level is an experience I never expected, and one I will carry with me my entire life.

About Darly Jamison

Darly Jamison is a midwestern girl who lived as a southern belle in a previous life. She's an award-winning author of contemporary romance, and she was once fired from the library for continuously reading on the job. When not writing, Darly can be found hanging out with her husband and children, or trying to perfect her chocolate-cheesecake recipe. Her debut novel, *Strawberry Wine*, was released by Kensington Publishing in 2017.

CHAPTER 24

The Wattys

ONE AWARD TO RULE THEM ALL

By Kara Barbieri

On Wattpad: @Pandean

Believe the hype. As part of the world's largest online writing contest, a Watty Award is what every Wattpad writer dreams of winning.

Wattpad is a giant platform with hundreds of millions of stories available from a vast number of talented writers. The Watty Awards, also called the Wattys, are like the Oscars of Wattpad, recognizing diamonds in the rough, trailblazers, and many other unique works. Taking place annually, it's the largest online writing contest in the world. As of this writing, winning doesn't bring a cash prize, but it can launch a writer into the stratosphere. Previous Watty Awards winners have gone on to sign with traditional publishers, secure film adaptations, and more. Make no mistake: You want a Watty. Here's what you need to know.

ENTERING YOUR STORY

Entering could not be simpler. Simply add the appropriate Wattys tag to your story when the time comes for a new competition.

For example, entering the 2017 competition meant adding the #Wattys2017 tag to a story. That's it. Use the tag on as many of your stories as you'd like to enter.

As of this writing, submissions open in June and close in August, with winners selected a couple of months later. The stories must be published on Wattpad, and year-specific requirements are listed on the @TheWattys profile. Be sure to check the profile each year because the rules (and prizes!) are subject to change.

CATEGORIES

Each year, the Watty Awards categories are a little different. They can range from achievement in a certain genre to unique multimedia usage and hidden gems that deserve readers' attention.

Some categories require an additional tag in order to enter them. Make sure you note whether the category you're aiming for has a different tag. One of the wonderful things about using a standard tag is that it makes your novel available for all categories included in that tag. You don't need to choose between multiple categories if you think your novel fits into more than one category. What do those categories look like? In 2017, they included:

- **THE ORIGINALS:** Trailblazing stories that changed the game, defied genres, broke the rules, and became one-of-a-kind stories on Wattpad
- **THE RIVETING READS:** An award for those pulse-quickening, edge-of-your-seat stories that hooked readers start to finish
- **THE BREAKTHROUGHS:** Up-and-coming stories that deserve to be discovered
- **THE NEWCOMERS:** Specifically for new members who have joined after a certain date
- **THE STORYSMITHS:** An award for those who wowed the Wattpad team with their masterful style, plot, and character

- **THE TAP AWARD:** Specifically for those stories on Tap, Wattpad's suspenseful chat-stories app that hooked readers and made them shiver in anticipation

The list above featured only the categories from 2017. The categories in 2016 were different from the ones in 2015 and so on. The rotation makes sure everyone gets an opportunity to win, no matter the writer's genre, status, or popularity.

If you're not sure that your novel fits into any of the categories, don't worry. Tag your story according to the details from @TheWattys. You can't go wrong by at least trying, and there is no penalty if you don't win.

Conversely, if you can't choose between stories that you want to enter, why not choose them all? You're allowed to submit more than one story at a time for Wattys consideration.

WINNING THE WATTYS

Winning the Wattys can definitely give you a boost! Winners are more likely to be advertised on the site and put on lists of must-read books. This could attract readers, agents, publishers, and other opportunities.

If you happen to win a category—and all categories have multiple winners—you can expect your reads to skyrocket and your book to attract much more attention. You'll also get a special sticker that you can put onto your book cover that lets everyone know you've won a Watty.

Of course, one of the best things about winning is the sense of pride and accomplishment. You wrote that story, you created those characters, those words are yours and no one else's, and among hundreds of thousands of different entries, yours was considered great enough to win.

When I entered my novel *White Stag* in the 2016 Wattys, I wasn't expecting anything to happen. My novel had a decent following, but to me it wasn't anything super special. I was in for a surprise when I won in the Trailblazers category. In 2016, the Trailblazers category was for books that came from nothing and took Wattpad by storm. My book just happened to be one of those books. My fanbase and reads grew by the thousands and became more and more noticeable both on and off Wattpad.

A few months later, I had a traditional book deal with St. Martin's Press for *White Stag* and its sequels sitting in my lap! While that obviously isn't the story for everyone, it shows what can happen when you've won a Watty. I was also pretty new, having been on Wattpad for less than a year. Winning made me feel so honored because people liked my story and thought it was special regardless of its or my own popularity level. And because people loved it enough for it to win, that opened the door for many more people to read and enjoy it.

IMPROVING YOUR CHANCES

The same things that will make you a better Wattpad writer overall can only help your chances at a Watty.

First and foremost, continue practicing your craft as a writer. Wattpad has a number of helpful resources, from the critiques classified section to genre-based clubs and how-to guides on writing. Unlike many other contests, the Wattys are not cutthroat. Those who write on Wattpad are almost always willing to help out newer writers. Use these resources to learn more about world-building, the type of style you like to write in, clichés and how to avoid them, and how to make characters that jump off the page.

What else can you do? Well, you can continue entering the Wattys every year, even if you didn't win the previous year. Just because your entry wasn't picked on your first try doesn't mean that you've lost all your chances. If your story fits into a category and meets the requirements detailed on the @TheWattys profile, definitely continue to submit. Editing and improving your craft, along with a positive "don't give up" attitude, can really make a difference when the Wattys roll around again.

Talk to other members, and form friendships. Read other writers' works because then they'll be more likely to read yours and offer helpful critiques. These things might seem small, but becoming known for these good deeds within the community will give you the right kind of exposure: the kind that will help boost your book's popularity. While popularity isn't the main factor that determines whether someone wins a Watty, it may play a role if a writer is being considered for awards that spotlight rising works.

Be unique! Don't be afraid if you find yourself wanting to write a concept that you're unsure other people will like. Write what feels good to you, not necessarily what other people are writing, because your writing will be more genuine if you're devoted to the idea. Don't avoid topics that are harder to touch on or characters that are diverse. If it comes from the heart, then write it. Genuine, heartfelt ideas are more appealing to readers than a story that goes with the crowd.

White Stag became popular and won a Watty mainly because the novel was different from what people were used to reading. Don't be afraid to do something that is a bit out in left field, like adding multimedia to your story, choosing a cast for your characters, or engaging your readers with author's notes. If you have an idea that you think is unique, try it out. It can only help your story to stand out more.

Cover art is also important when it comes to the Wattys. While your story isn't going to be chosen based on cover art alone, great cover art can catch the eyes of those mysterious judges and pull them into your story in the same way that the covers of physical books can pique your interest. While you shouldn't necessarily judge a book by its cover, covers are still wonderful tools that say something about the books they grace. In some categories that are focused on media, having a great cover shows that you know what you're doing. If you're not familiar with how to create a cover on Wattpad, check out the section covering that topic in this book.

Most importantly, remember that this is supposed to be a fun experience. It's a chance for you and many other writers to get your book out there, win, and get exposure—but you shouldn't take it too seriously either. Not winning a Watty doesn't mean your book is bad or poorly written, and it doesn't mean that no one likes it. Thousands of books are entered into the Wattys every year, and they can only pick a few winners per category. So if your book isn't picked, that doesn't reflect poorly on you as a writer.

The Wattys should be a fun experience meant to build up writers, not tear them down. While it is a competition, you should treat other members who enter with the respect and courtesy they deserve, and congratulate the winners. At the end of the day, you are all creators of wonderful works. Building each other up and making the community stronger is more important than winning an award. Wattpad is a community bent on learning while growing as writers and making friends throughout that process. That's what matters most.

HOW DOES WATTPAD CHOOSE THE WINNERS?

As of this writing, the exact process is still under wraps, but a post by @TheWattys suggests what many already expected: Data science plays a significant role. The following is from that post.

"In the context of The Wattys, data science means that we (the team at Wattpad administering the awards) spend time understanding, from a quantitative as well as a qualitative perspective, which features or variables can be used to identify the stories that match a particular set of contest criteria in a meaningful way."

Let's pretend that we created an award called Fan Love. Through content experts and our data, we know that the more time that someone spends reading, commenting, and voting on a story, the greater the correlation there is to what we have determined is "fan love."

When we're creating a data-science approach to evaluating the entries, we develop an algorithm that takes all these variables into consideration (although we might weigh one higher than another). And it's in this way that we are able to discover the most promising content in our community. Our editorial team then reviews each story individually.

Here are some key elements that help our editorial team highlight promising stories:

- **CHARACTER**—You main character is your driver. We need to love him or love to hate him if we are going to let him take us on a journey.
- **HOOK**—Your idea is your golden ticket. Give us a hook that we can sink our teeth into, like a unique concept or a new spin on a beloved cliché.
- **VOICE**—Your narrative voice is your multi-tool. If you use it well, we, the readers, are putty in your hands. This is where writers show off their creative artistry by weaving ordinary words into something magical.
- **WORLD**—While great world-building doesn't have to be complicated, it should be specific, clear, and logical within the scope of your story. Give us too little, and we're lost. Give us too much, and we're buried under details.
- **STAKES**—Stakes give us something to lose if we don't hold on to every single word. The writers who manage to grip us right from the get-go are the ones we're least likely to forget.

WATTY MYTHS

On a site so large and active as Wattpad, there are bound to be a few myths and misconceptions about the Wattys that may stress out a new writer and make her feel like winning is impossible. To ease some minds, I will now dispel a few myths about the Wattys.

1. **"I HAVE TO BE POPULAR IN ORDER TO WIN."**

You don't have to be popular in order to win the Wattys. Unlike a lot of contests on the internet—writing or otherwise—the Wattys are not decided by who has the most reads or votes. A team of people from the Wattpad HQ and data mined from the site determine how the Wattys winners are chosen. That means that whether you're a Wattpad Star or an undiscovered gem, you're eligible to win.

2. **"I WON'T WIN IF I WRITE [INSERT GENRE HERE]."**

No matter what type of story you write, there will always be a place for it in the Wattys. From paranormal to teen fiction and short story, all have a chance to win. Every year the categories for the Wattys change a bit, making new opportunities for your stories. A lot of the categories aren't genre based. Instead, they tend to be based more on the writing, presentation, or uniqueness of the story. So you won't have to worry about finding a category for your vampire-romance novel. All genres have a chance at each category.

3. **"IF MY STORY IS RATED 'MATURE,' IT WON'T WIN."**

On Wattpad, stories are rated "Mature" if they have graphic violence, sex, or drug use. Depending on the story, suicide and self-harm or certain types of abuse might also need this rating. The rating depends more on the way the story is written than on the subjects in the story.

Mature stories aren't shown on the Hot Lists. However, readers can still find them using the search bar. The Hot List is a great way to get people's attention, but it isn't everything. The Wattys allow both mature and non-mature stories to enter and win. Ranking (or lack thereof) on the Hot List doesn't guarantee that a writer will win or lose.

4. **"WINNING THE WATTYS WON'T HELP A NEW WRITER GET EXPOSURE."**

Winning the Wattys is not reserved for established writers, and neither are the perks of winning. Both long-term and new members will gain exposure through their wins, and there are even categories specifically for newer writers. As with established Wattpad writers, new writers' winning stories are advertised on the @TheWattys profile page. They also get a special sticker for their covers, signifying that the story won a Watty. When I won my Watty for *White Stag*, I had not even been on Wattpad a year. I still got a lot of exposure for my work, and my read count quickly doubled.

WHAT DO YOU HAVE TO LOSE?

So, what are you waiting for? When the Wattys come around, enter your work into the competition. I can promise that you won't be sorry you did.

About Kara Barbieri

Kara Barbieri, known as @Pandean on Wattpad, is the author of *White Stag*, which will be released in winter 2019 by St. Martin's Press. She lives with her four cats and two dogs, twirls a fire staff, and has a passion for goats.

CHAPTER 25

Wattpad Labs

REDEFINING STORYTELLING WITH TAP BY WATTPAD

By Jo Watson

On Wattpad: @JoWatson_101

Experiment with the innovative (and free) Tap app to discover new ways to supplement Wattpad stories or create new ones.

LIGHTING A FIRE

Four years ago, I stumbled upon a writing contest taking place on a platform I'd never heard of before. This unique platform allowed anyone to become an author. No longer was book writing reserved for the intelligentsia and the literary glitterati. It was for everyone. And it was free to read! This blew me away. The concept was so revolutionary that I knew immediately I wanted to be part of it. This was the future of storytelling.

And so I jumped on board. Little did I know that my jump would be a leap into a whole new career as a professional author. The day I pressed "Publish" on the first chapter of my first book, *Burning Moon*, my entire life changed. I ended up winning that competition, and the ball started rolling. *And oh, how it has rolled!*

I now have an agent in New York, publishing deals, thirty million reads on Wattpad, and more awards. Thanks to Wattpad, I've become a full-time author, a dream I know so many other writers wish to fulfill. And just when I thought the ball couldn't possibly roll anymore, that my career couldn't get any better, more interesting, or exciting, I discovered Tap by Wattpad Labs.

ENTER TAP

That same feeling I got four years ago was upon me once more. Entire stories told through text messaging? That same thought hit me: *This is the future of storytelling.* I could see with such clarity the potential for this kind of storytelling. As someone who has written in mediums such as plays, films, ads, radio dramas, features, and novels, the idea of telling stories in a completely different way excited me beyond belief.

So, with no real knowledge of how it all worked, I pressed "Publish" once more. And soon people started reading so much that in only six months, I have written more than twenty-nine stories, been "tapped" (read) more than twenty million times, and won a Watty Award. A whole new way of telling stories opened up to me, and my career grew—again, thanks to Wattpad.

Today, when people ask me what I do for a living, I tell them that I'm an author of books and interactive stories. That is how integral I see chat stories being to my career and future as an author. Storytelling is evolving at such a rapid pace at the moment, and Tap stories are just one of the new forms it has taken on. I think we're at a very exciting time in history, and we would be remiss if we did not jump on board and ride the new, exciting storytelling wave.

TAPPING 101
What Are Tap Stories, and Why Are They Popular?

To put it simply, Tap stories are told through the medium of text messaging, with interactive elements, like images, video, and multiple-choice options that play out between two or more characters. I often draw a parallel between chat stories and reality TV. Reading a chat story gives you that same voyeuristic kick as watching a bunch of plastic surgery–enhanced housewives bicker over a man. It's eavesdropping on someone's private conversation. You become the ultimate fly on the wall. And let's be honest, who doesn't love that? I think this is a big part of Tap stories' appeal and has definitely contributed to their rise in popularity. Another factor that makes them engaging is that they play out one text message at a time. To see the next text message in the series, you simply tap on the screen.

To draw another parallel, think of the TV show *24*, an action-adventure show where each season played out in "real time" over the course of twenty-four one-hour episodes. Consequently, the show was nail-bitingly fast-paced and suspenseful. Well, a Tap story is very similar in that respect. A good Tap story has the ability to reach out, grab your attention, and then keep you hooked and on the edge of your seat until the very end. Reading an interactive story gives you a front-row seat as the action plays out in real time. The other appeal of Tap stories lies in their unique ability to provide you with a bite-sized piece of entertainment on the go. They're bits of takeout entertainment delivered straight to the device in your hand.

What Is the Tap App All About?

Tap by Wattpad is a very user-friendly app that allows you to create your own chat stories. The app itself is free, as of this writing, but it comes with a limited number of "taps." You have the option of upgrading to a paid premium subscription (with a seven-day free-trial period), and you can cancel anytime. This gives you access to interactive elements and media, such as pictures and video, as well as unlimited reading.

How to Create a Tap Story

Creating a Tap story is as easy as having a text-message conversation with your friends. The app is also very simple; take it from someone who is not tech savvy. Here are the steps to creating and publishing your first story:

1. Download the Tap app from any app store.
2. Sign up for a free trial, and then create your Tap account and user profile.
3. In your profile, click on "New Story" to start creating.

That's it! Follow the prompts to create characters, scenes, and texts, and finally, hit "Publish." This entire process might only take a few minutes, especially if you already have a story idea in mind.

What Works on Tap?

Two genres stand out as being the most popular on Tap: horror and romance. After horror and romance, the top genres (as of this writing) are comedy, science fiction, and fantasy, in that order. When one reads some of the most popular stories on Tap, it's easy to see why they've captured people's imaginations. Again, it's all about that voyeuristic aspect, feeling like you're right there with the characters as they fall in love, dodge the serial killer, or get eaten by a demon. The reader is with the characters every step of the way as they live through the terror or joy of each moment.

To maximize your reads, keep in mind your readers' demographics. Tap readers are primarily women between thirteen and twenty-eight years old. So when creating Tap stories, regardless of your chosen genre, try to write stories that might appeal to this group of readers.

Creating Characters Worth Caring About

Character is still king, even in short text stories. Writing text-message stories doesn't give us license to forget or abandon the fundamentals of good, solid storytelling. It's easy to make a chainsaw-wielding psycho come after your main character, but if you haven't crafted a character who readers care about, they're not going to give a damn about his upcoming decapitation!

When writing chat stories, I usually do a very brief character setup; this can be as short as two lines. I use a smattering of small talk to establish characters' traits and relationships. This would be especially important if a conversation involves more than two people. You would want to take a few moments to establish each character's unique voice. Giving each character a distinct voice makes dialogue easier for the reader to follow, especially if messages are being fired back and forth in the heat of a moment. Strong character voices can elevate a decent story to unforeseen heights.

In my most popular story, "Selfie," I established a loving, flirty relationship between a couple before I ripped it all away from them. This approach makes the reader much more emotionally invested in the characters and their story. It's very tempting to jump right into the action, and sometimes this is necessary, but it's also important to consider taking a moment to flesh out your characters and color in their worlds.

Create a Story That Captivates

Chat stories are a unique medium, so how do we write them? There are a few keys to writing good chat stories, and one of them is "the hook." Preferably within the first few messages, catch the reader's attention with something that will make it impossible to stop reading. It could be a creepy plot element, an interesting character, or something bizarre that makes her want to read further.

Another key to a good Tap story is pace. We need to get in and out of the action quickly. These are short stories, so we need to keep them moving. Thus far, the data has shown that (although this does seem to keep evolving as more and more readers use Tap) the sweet spot for a story's duration is somewhere between two and four minutes. You will be able to see your minute count once your story is published. To stay within the preferred length parameters, try to create stories that are between 140 and 200 lines. But don't let this suggestion stifle or limit your creativity either.

In addition, when writing a chat story, consider the weight of action vs. conversation. Don't fall into the trap of thinking that a chat story is just that, "having a chat," because that isn't always the case. There needs to be something happening in the scene; the chat part often occurs as a result of this action. While reading a conversation can be entertaining and does work well for some genres, like humor, that don't necessarily rely on action, it's always a good idea to get your characters up and moving.

Write Believable Dialogue

Keeping your dialogue believable is key to writing successful Tap stories. As someone who studied playwriting and has worked in TV, I'd be remiss if I didn't share one of the best pieces of advice I ever got: "Read it out loud" (even if doing so makes you look like an idiot). This is by far the best way to check whether you're writing naturalistic dialogue. Hearing what you've written makes it easy to identify where the conversation feels stilted and contrived. Don't worry about correct grammar and punctuation in dialogue, especially in Tap stories. This is the one place where you can chuck all those rules. Not many people use correct punctuation when texting.

When we talk about dialogue in the context of a chat story, we're really referring to the actual messages and how they're constructed. It's important that messages look realistic, so parent characters should write correctly (for the most part), while thirteen-year-olds texting with friends shld txt short anc quick, possibly with spelling errors. Feel free to substitute emojis for verbal emotional expression or replies to questions, and don't forget to use the popular acronyms and abbreves (abbreviations) that are synonymous with text talk. Think "WTH," "LOL," and "IDK" ("what the hell," "laugh out loud," and "I don't know"). Tap is less forgiving than other platforms when it comes to stilted dialogue because it's voyeuristic and plays out one text at a time.

This might sound silly, but considering your demographics, it's a good idea to learn the current text lingo. The language used online and in chat communications is constantly changing, with new abbreviations and acronyms popping up all the time. If you don't have access to an actual living teenager, use Google to keep abreast of trends.

Overall, the dialogue must serve the greater purpose of the story, especially within the realm of Tap. Keep it snappy. There's no space for waffling. Dialogue must get to the point and push the story forward.

Moreover, keeping sentences short and sweet is wise from a technical perspective. If you do have a longer one, break it up into multiple messages. There's no harm in making the same character type three messages in a row. This is only irritating in real life when you're trying to have a conversation with that person who writes two words per line! Lastly, there's no need to put "quotation marks" around text dialogue.

Media on Tap

Inserting media into Tap is yet another way to further enliven your story. As of this writing, users can insert pictures into their stories. The option for video and sound insertion is available in beta but only to some writers. This will expand and change in the future since Tap is an ever-evolving platform, so be sure to use the most recent version of the app. Using media really brings the Tap experience to life, creating a completely immersive story that engages your senses and uses your mobile device to its full potential.

DID TAP MAKE ME A BETTER WRITER?

Surprisingly, the answer is "Yes!" I know some "real writers" rolled their eyes at me when I told them what I was doing, but the truth is that chat-story writing has had a positive impact on my novel writing. Tap is a fast-paced, shorthanded way to tell stories. It forces you to cut to the chase, remove all the fluff, and jump straight in. Tap writing made me evaluate my verbose nature and forced me to look for quicker, more effective ways to reveal characters' backstories. Furthermore, it has definitely improved my dialogue writing, which has become more free and natural. It has even helped me communicate better with my teenage cousin!

PUSHING THE BOUNDS OF CREATIVITY WITH TAP

From text messages to your pets to chats with your future self to conversations between Beyoncé's unborn twins and conversations with characters from your books, Tap allows you to push the boundaries of storytelling in the most imaginative ways possible. The sky is the limit when it comes to what you can do in this medium, and that's one of the things I find incredibly exciting about chat stories.

Tap is a great way to enrich your Wattpad experience. I've used the app to create bonus scenes featuring characters' text message exchanges, which I've then linked to within my Wattpad stories. I'm also experimenting with using Tap to write an entire book, a sequel to a popular Wattpad novel. Writers could even flip the process around and use Tap as a testing ground for full-length Wattpad novels. In the future, developers are looking to facilitate integration of Tap and Wattpad stories. By embracing this new technology, you can expand your fanbase and build your author brand.

Recommended Tap Reading

- *Hide* for nail-biting horror and excellent use of media
- *Molly* for the choose-your-own-ending style
- *Accidental Confession* for fun, young, flirty romance
- *Virtual Boyfriend* for creative storytelling
- *Single Like a Pringle* for humor
- *#LivePoliceStop* for an intense live stream video immersive experience
- *Accidental Stylist* for choose-your-own-adventure humor
- *Prosper* for dark science fiction
- *Bro Down, Lawyer Up* (written by *Rick and Morty* creator Dan Harmon) for political satire

GIVE IT A SHOT

Since you're already writing on Wattpad, give Tap a try. Download the free app, and start experimenting. Wattpad's suite of apps is there to offer tools, not rules. Don't be shy. Put yourself out there, and see what happens.

About Jo Watson

Jo Watson is a two-time Watty Award winner and a member of the Tap Squad. She is the published author of the Destination Love series, a screenwriter, and sometimes a playwright living in South Africa, where she is probably listening to Depeche Mode.

PART 4

Inspiration

CHAPTER 26

Words of Wisdom for Wattpad Writers

By Benjamin Sobieck

On Wattpad: @BenSobieck

You've heard it all before. It's still true.

TIME TO QUIT?

Whether you're new to Wattpad or staked your claim a while ago, at some point, you're going to have a bad day as a writer. That bad day will be followed by another, then another, and yet another, and eventually, you'll start to wonder if you're cut out for the Wattpad experience. This is as understandable as it is inevitable, which is why there's also an understandable and inevitable response: Don't give up. It's almost too simple, to the point of seeming condescending. You might think, *Don't give up? I put three years into a story no one read, buddy. The smart money is on giving up.*

Well, I've got news for you. There are a lot of smart people out there who no one's heard of because they give in to thoughts like those above. As a writer, you work in the illogical all the time. Ignoring practical advice should be nothing new for you. Otherwise, you'd be reading a guide to tax accounting, not Wattpad. How do you think most of the writers featured in this book became

Wattpad Stars? No matter what, they kept going, as if they knew they'd eventually find traction. And they did.

The more I play the writing game, the more I see that this is the constant common denominator. I'm not dismissing raw talent, but there is an exit ramp at a certain station in life that separates those who become "real writers" and those who drop out because the ROI isn't clear. And it has nothing to do with talent. I'm talking in tangible, pragmatic terms here. In my world, this exodus happened around age thirty, and it came with the responsibilities of family and career. Writers in my age group started dropping off the radar en masse, leaving only the very desperate and the very delusional (i.e., me) to keep pounding at the keyboards in the hope of making something stick. Now I'm honored to be the editor of this book, and I'm happy to say that it's only part of my résumé, not the whole thing.

My tepid peers sometimes ask how I manage to have both a life and be a writer, as though they were two separate things. It's yet another understandable and inevitable question, with the same sort of answer: I didn't give up. You might pass that exit ramp at a different time or station in life, but you'll know it when you're the only one left in the room.

These things matter to writing at large, but it's especially important to keep in mind for Wattpad because everything is so public. If you're feeling down on yourself and not writing, everyone will know it. If you're struggling to keep a positive attitude, everyone will know it. If you're on the brink of giving up, everyone will know it. If you write while wearing a ratty T-shirt and leprechaun socks and you've stared at the coffee-ring stains so long that they look like they're talking to you, everyone will know it.

Well, maybe not that last one. There are advantages to working in solitude. The point is that maintaining forward momentum is key to making something happen on Wattpad. Wattpad, by design, rewards the authors who keep writing. That's all there is to it.

INSPIRATION TO KEEP GOING

I might be 50 percent nuts 100 percent of the time, but I'm not the only one to pick up on this. How do I know? I asked. 2016 Watty Award winner Michael Estrin (@mestrin) believes that "every writer in the history of writing has felt that way [giving up] at some point." He's not wrong. In fact, I'd say that doubt is the reason that a writer keeps evolving. If you think that your writing is perfect, you'll never seek out ways to improve.

Wattpad Star M. Kane (@Toxic_Wonderland) keyed into a common solution: "I take a step back to remember why I started writing that particular story in the first place. That's usually enough to keep me going, but other times I end up leaving it alone for a week or two. Going back and looking at something with fresh eyes can do a world of good." I might call that the zombie method: Kill it, bury it, dig it up, and bring it back to life; repeat as necessary. Aim for the head! The undead aside, Ariel Klontz (@arielklontz), another Wattpad Star, offered a wider perspective that likely resonates with many WIPs: "Rome wasn't built in a day."

YOU'RE IN GOOD COMPANY

No, Rome wasn't built in a day. However, you're still here reading this and have the chance to see the results of your hard work. You know who wasn't? F. Scott Fitzgerald.

Although he is not on Wattpad and could not be reached for comment, Fitzgerald is worth mentioning here because he died before his seminal work, *The Great Gatsby*, arguably *the* great American novel, became the classic it is known as today. Upon initial publication in 1925, *The Great Gatsby* marvelously bombed with both critics and readers. Fitzgerald's life only got worse from there, and he went to his grave in 1940 thinking that *Gatsby* was an abject failure.

By a stroke of luck, the novel found its second life during World War II. In the United States, the Council on Books in Wartime (yes, a real thing) distributed millions of books to United States military personnel. One of those titles was *The Great Gatsby*. A new generation of readers ate the book up, and the rest is history. You never know what could happen, but you know what won't happen if you quit writing.

"I STARTED WRITING ON WATTPAD, BUT NOTHING IS HAPPENING"

I hear this after giving presentations about Wattpad at writing conferences, and it's a perfectly reasonable gripe. The writer in question is usually doing a good job of staying active, but for whatever reason, readers just haven't been receptive. Seeing as how I enjoy the present positions of my teeth, the standard "Just keep writing" advice won't do. Instead, I say that Wattpad is a *slow burn*, and I say that for reasons other than self-preservation. It's true. There are no overnight success stories. Traction usually builds exponentially. Are there writers who take off faster than others? Sure, but what does that have to do with you?

If that's not convincing, look at it from the other side. Someone, somewhere, is playing the Wattpad game from a mile behind where you are right now. They're struggling to catch up to *you*. You're already living someone else's goal. You made it. Now keep going. Better days are ahead of you.

"I'M NOT MAKING ANY MONEY DOING THIS"

That's likely true. On Wattpad, only a select few can win cash prizes through contests or participate in a branded campaign. Converting Wattpad followers into book buyers somewhere else can also be challenging (although the excellent tips in this guide should better your odds). Here's the thing about monetizing audiences on or off Wattpad: If you can get enough people to pay attention to you in a predictable way, you can make money. That's true of this century and any other. Influencer marketing isn't just for Twitter celebrities and YouTube personalities. If you have an audience, you can get a sponsor. If you can get a sponsor, you can make money.

The trick is that, unlike the official Wattpad initiatives, no one is going to hand that to you. You may have to query a company in the same way you'd query an agent or publisher. You may offer to work product placements into stories. You might shoot a certain link to your followers. You're going to have to sell yourself one way or another.

However, making money should be a *side effect* of what you're doing, not your raison d'être. To look at it otherwise is to use the wrong metric. If chapter one makes $100 and chapter two makes $99, is the first really better than the second?

"I DON'T WANT TO BE TOO SUCCESSFUL ON WATTPAD"

Does success on Wattpad preclude other opportunities? No. Millions of reads on Wattpad is *proof* to those holding the keys of opportunity that you're deserving. This is a good problem to have, so it's no reason to throw in the towel.

AND IF YOU'RE NOT INSPIRED YET …

When I'm feeling frustrated with my writing progress, I like to remind myself of the bigger picture. Not just about my life's work but about writing itself. Bear with me. This is a little out there. There is no logical reason for your writing to exist. You could trace the components that make up your keyboard back to the Big Bang, but there is no such trail leading back to a source for your writing. Sure, there are ideas you've picked up through life, but they weren't the story itself. The farther back down the trail you go, the less clear things become. Eventually, you hit a wall. Try it with one of your stories. Work backward, starting with a key character, plot, or story element. Ask yourself where it came from, and repeat that question when you receive an answer. Eventually, you'll hit a deep, dark void where all you can do is shrug your shoulders. It's spooky.

You are creating something, a story, literally from nothing. You weren't born with the thoughts that started to form the shape of your stories. They emerged from within the vacuum inside your head that contained exactly zero percent of the words in your books. In the beginning of a story's life, there are no thoughts. Then comes the flickering of thoughts. Those mash together to form a complete idea, and that's telegraphed through your fingertips. If there is such a thing as magic, this is it.

Despite bending the rules of logic, you're here anyway, typing on your keyboards and your devices, describing things that don't exist to people you'll probably never meet who are across rocky roads of time and space. With Wattpad, you're doing that in a way that no one else in history has had the opportunity to do. How rare and fortunate you are to even consider writing on something like Wattpad. I don't know about you, but this perspective puts me back into shape for writing. It widens the fences, and I don't feel as trapped by my own ambitions. No longer am I stuck competing with myself. I'm participating in something much bigger than my story.

GO HAVE FUN

If there's one constant to the tips in this book, it's that Wattpad should above all be a fun experience. If nothing else, you can at least have that.

FUTHER READING

Don't stop now! Continue learning how to get the most out of your writing with the Wattpad Writers' Portal at wattpad.com/writers.

INDEX

engagements, 190

Writer's Guide to Wattpad

WRITER'S DIGEST

ONLINEworkshops
WritersOnlineWorkshops.*com*

Our workshops combine the best of world-class writing instruction with the convenience and immediacy of the Web to create a state-of-the-art learning environment. You get all of the benefits of a traditional workshop setting—peer review, instructor feedback, a community of writers, and productive writing practice—without any of the hassle.

EMPOWER YOUR WRITING WITH CRAFT & COMMUNITY

Author in Progress

BY THERESE WALSH, EDITOR, AND THE MEMBERS OF WRITER UNBOXED

Author in Progress is the perfect no-nonsense guide for excelling at every step of the novel-writing process, from setting goals, researching, and drafting to giving and receiving critiques, polishing prose, and seeking publication.

Available from WritersDigestShop.com and your favorite book retailers.